A SCHOOL SECURITY OFFICER

A SCHOOL SECURITY OFFICER

WHAT MAKES A GOOD ONE?

James Puckett

ARCHWAY
PUBLISHING

Archway Publishing books may be ordered through booksellers or by contacting:

Archway Publishing
1663 Liberty Drive
Bloomington, IN 47403
www.archwaypublishing.com
1-(888)-242-5904

ISBN: 978-1-4808-1163-8 (sc)
ISBN: 978-1-4808-1164-5 (e)

Library of Congress Control Number: 2014917427

Printed in the United States of America.

Archway Publishing rev. date: 10/28/2014

Contents

DEDICATION

Dedicated to all past, present, and future school security officers who have committed their lives to help make schools a safer place for children to learn.

To all law enforcement personnel who have assisted us in making school a safer place for children to learn.

Dedicated to all past, present, and future educators who have committed their lives to educating children to ensure they have an opportunity to live a successful life.

To all school counselors, secretaries, food service workers, and custodial staff who have been instrumental in helping make my job easier.

Foreword

By Phil Keit
Former Knoxville Police Chief

A School Security Officer: What Makes A Good One? is written by an experienced and motivated professional to guide the preparation, thinking, compassion and professional performance of current and future school security officers. The unique manner in the way the author approaches the topic of not only choosing a career as a school security officer, but the recipe essential for success, provides the reader the core competencies required to go from good to great in their performance. The text fills the gap between formalized initial training and what the school security officer must understand and prepare for, and to perform as a professional. Communities and schools have a common expectation of making the environment in schools *one that is safe for teachers to teach and children to learn;* and, although simply stated, is very difficult and challenging to make the expectations a true reality. This text provides an easy to read, motivational opportunity for current and future school security officers, with emphasis on key behaviors, performance and professional knowledge. These three key competencies are provided in a straightforward manner on how a school security officer must have the professional knowledge through provided and self-provided training and education, coupled with the behavior and professionalism to demonstrate compassion and commitment to the role of the school security officer. Schools are often described as a microcosm of society as a whole. However, in an ever changing society complete with violence, absence of principles and civility, our schools must fill the societal void through education and behavior modification of future children. Critical to the education and behavior modification of children is the school security officer. Just as our personal experiences have reminded us of who was our best teacher or best coach, the school security officer will be equally remembered. The author emphasizes preparation to perform, fairness with firmness, optics matter, and self-discipline and self-development are required to establish a fundamental foundation to be considered and remembered as the "best school security officer". Woven throughout the text is the reminder that possessing only a few of the requirements could suffice to be a status quo performer, but rather the harnessing of all the skills, behaviors, and performance with commitment will make a successful school security officer. The role of the school security officer is not for the meek, weak or uncompassionate, but rather a career commitment to protect, guide and defend children so teachers can provide the educational opportunities to give every child an opportunity at the American dream of being a contributing and successful citizen.

Introduction

Being a school security officer! You may ask, "What's so difficult about being a school security officer?" Or, "What makes a good school security officer?" And, "Why would you feel compelled to write on such a subject?" To answer the first question, this is not a book that focuses merely on the duties and responsibilities of a school security officer but more on what it takes for a school security officer to carry out those duties and responsibilities effectively. I neither claim to be an expert in this area, nor do I have a degree in criminal justice. I have no prior law enforcement background. But I have learned some things in the past eight years about being a school security officer, and what it takes to be a good one. All professions and careers carry with them a certain level of ethics, hard work, and toughness.

A school security officer is no different. A school security officer must possess certain qualities, traits, and characteristics that many other professions and jobs don't require. With the rise in crime and violence in our cities, communities, and schools, security officers or guards are in high demand. And they must be good ones. Since 1997 there have been 382 school shootings in forty-two different states (http://www.stoptheshootings.org/ n.d.).

The men and women who have been charged with the responsibility of protecting our children in schools must do it with the promptness, willingness, and readiness necessary to keep children and staff safe. This is not a job to be taken lightly. This is a huge responsibility for you to carry out. If you're considering a career as a school security officer, you should really put some serious thought into the huge responsibility that comes with it.

In today's society, you can find a security officer or guard in places where they would not have been found ten, or even five years ago. It's unfortunate that armed security officers are needed in many public schools today, but this is where we are as a society. If there continues to be a demand for armed school security officers in the future, and there will be, they should strive to not only be good ones, but the best they can be. They should be highly trained and equipped to do whatever is necessary to provide safety and security at the school where they work. Anything less than *good* is unacceptable. But the ultimate goal is to be their very *best*.

Serving as an armed school security officer for the past eight years has helped me gain even greater respect for law enforcement personnel. I have great respect for the men and women of law enforcement who have dedicated themselves and taken an oath to protect and serve when duty calls. Those I have had the pleasure of serving with over the past eight years have been nothing but professional in their duties and responsibilities. Sometimes I wonder what our communities, cities, and schools would be like were it not for them. To all the law enforcement personnel who have served and are still serving, I would like to say, thank you. This book is not intended to show comparisons or contrasts between school security officers and law enforcement personnel—even though there are several—but to outline some of the qualities all school security officers must have in order to be effective at carrying out their duties and responsibilities.

Even though our duties and responsibilities are different we both must possess a certain work ethic and mental toughness, which are vital in our line of work. Both school security officers and law enforcement officers must have a *good* work ethic and *good* personal characteristics in order to be *good* at their job. When I use the word "good" I mean more than just doing enough to get by. I mean doing whatever it takes to show others that you're serious about your job. "Good" means having the qualities that are desirable or distinguishing in a particular thing or area. To me, good is not just being average, but performing at a level that is above average. A lot of people are fine with average-level performance in their duties and responsibilities. I desire to perform above average working as a school security officer.

Average performance is for the average-thinking person. I am by no means an average-thinking person. I have high standards for whatever I'm called to do. I work and do my best. It's good in my book when I've done my best. Believe it or not, I've been criticized by certain people for my hard work ethic and promptness in getting things done. So don't be surprised when you do your best at your job and others who are average in their thinking and work ethic complain about your high level of performance.

Often when law enforcement personnel get called out or dispatched to a location where a crime has been reported, or even on a routine call, they don't know what to expect. The only information they have is what the dispatcher has relayed to them. Even though most of the times they have limited information on the calls they receive, they still go about their duties and responsibilities answering those calls. Law enforcement personnel can never predict the outcome when they pull over a vehicle for a traffic violation or arrive at a house where a domestic dispute has been reported. Many have lost their lives just by performing a routine traffic stop, answering a family domestic call, or by simply serving a warrant (National Law Enforcement Officers Memorial Fund (2014, April 14) Retrieved from http:// www.nleomf. org/facts/officer-fatalities-data/year.html).

School security officers don't make traffic stops, go out on domestic or burglary calls, or perform the other duties that law enforcement personnel perform. Instead, we perform our duties entirely at the school level. We monitor the flow of traffic on campus, and enforce the school's traffic policy and parking rules. We are not necessarily held to an oath, but I feel I'm under an oath every minute of every day. I mentally hold myself to an oath to protect and serve the students and staff where I work.

During sporting events, school security officers come in contact with people from other communities and students from other schools. Some school security officers are also tasked with the duty of directing traffic before and after school, which is a challenge in itself. I view school security officers as customer service representatives—we are there to serve students, staff, and parents. Unlike most customer service personnel, we are not there to make people happy or please them (at least, that is not our ultimate goal), but to maintain safety and security. If they are happy in the process, then it's good for everyone.

A phrase I will use throughout this book is: *If you don't make yourself visible, it's just like you're not there.* Being visible is important, but being watchful and engaged while being visible is even more important. In my career as a school security officer, I've learned that most students, especially the ones looking to do mischief, will look around to see if security or other staff members are watching. I'm not suggesting that you'll see every little thing that takes place, but just being present so these students know you're close by will deter a great deal of trouble. Nevertheless, there may be times and places when you deem it necessary to keep your whereabouts discreet. Even when this may be necessary, you must be vigilant in looking and listening, and be ready to respond at a moment's notice. In my years serving as a school security officer, I've found that being visible to students and others was the best deterrent of potential trouble.

Some final words: This book will address how I believe a school security officer should conduct himself or herself in order to carry out their assigned duties and responsibilities effectively, and the qualities and characteristics he or she must possess. It doesn't contain an all-inclusive list, but shows what has helped me become successful in my career as a school security officer. There will probably be things you read in this book that rub you the wrong way or make you feel uncomfortable. I don't write these things to offend anyone, or to question their ability to do their job. I write this book to bring attention to some of the challenges I've experienced and observed while serving as a school security officer and how I dealt with them.

My hope is that this book will help already good school security officers become better school security officers. This book is meant to encourage school security officers and those who work similar jobs. The goal is to offer some helpful suggestions to help them be more confident and efficient in their duties and responsibilities—advice on how to be better than average. My own work ethic is neither average nor mediocre. I've never liked doing things "just enough to get by." To me, a person who only produces average or mediocre work says, "I'm only willing to do so much, and don't expect any more out of me."

Being average or mediocre will not get you the promotion you think you deserve. Employers are looking for employees who will take their work ethic and habits beyond average or mediocre to over and above the standard.

I've had many jobs in my lifetime. In each one of them, even as far back as working in the fields as the son of sharecroppers in the deep south of Tennessee in the mid-sixties, I've always done my very best at every job, task, and responsibility I was given. I've carried this attitude and work ethic with me up to this very day. I don't think I could perform any differently if I tried. It's a good feeling knowing that I've done my very best, and never settled for just being average. I hope that after you have read this entire book, you'll understand how to make the improvements necessary in your own work ethic.

Some have called me a perfectionist. I would say to them, "I'm not perfect. I just want to be good at what I've chosen to do." I will never be the best at anything, but at least I can try to be *my* best at what I've chosen to do. As a school security officer, you owe your best to the people you serve. If this makes you uncomfortable, perhaps you should consider a different career. I write these things not to point out flaws or address someone else's failures, because I too have flaws and have made many mistakes. Rather, I write this book to help you in your job as a school security officer. I'm sure that if you read this book with an open mind, you'll agree that there's at least one thing you would like to change about the way you operate as a school security officer. Working in school security is not a *hard* job. It can be very stressful at times, but you should not allow the stress to interfere with your job. You must still take your duties and responsibilities seriously and work at them diligently. While you're on duty there will be plenty of slack time, but never down time.

Whether you're a young school security officer just starting on the job, or a seasoned one who has been on the job for several years, this book can benefit you in carrying out your duties and responsibilities. It can help you become a good school security officer on your way to becoming a better one. This book is for all present and future school security officers.

Notes

CHAPTER ONE

A School Security Officer Must Be Tough

School security officers might have to perform a variety of jobs, so physical fitness is important. Just as important, we must also be mentally tough. The right mindset is vital for completing your duties and assigned tasks. Speaking from experience, mental toughness is crucial for getting the job done. Some days, students are less than nice, and say very unpleasant things about me and to me. Some parents are not always happy to see me, and have some very unconstructive, choice words as part of their greeting. Some parents and students even go as far as to send me letters and cards telling me how unfair, prejudiced, and racist I am…all untrue. At times I've just wanted to quit.

Many days, I walk around the school saying, "I'm going to retire. I don't have to take this abuse." Sometimes I wonder why they would treat the "good guy" so badly. Those are the days when my mental toughness is challenged. Having thick skin as a school security officer is not an option; if your goal is to be a good one—one that will last through the fire and rain, or at least the school year—it's a necessity. Certainly, there are days when it seems like what I do makes no difference, and I'm not appreciated by some of those people I'm serving. Still, my love for children and the people I serve is the driving force that brings me back year after year.

A school security officer is a servant to the staff, students, parents, and people who visit the school campus. One would think that all students and parents would treat someone who has been tasked to be a servant, protector, and guard with the utmost respect and honor. This is not so for a school security officer. Many students and parents will not look upon you as someone they respect. Some people think that most security officers sit at a desk all day and look at cameras on monitor screens, but this is not true for school security officers. Each officer's duties and responsibilities can vary depending on the type of school he or she is assigned to. But every officer, whether assigned to an elementary school, middle school, or high school, has one common responsibility—to establish and maintain safety and security throughout the entire school and its campus. Since this one common responsibility will require that we perform many tasks, toughness is essential. Without this basic characteristic, a person working as a school security officer will not last long, nor will they be able to be good at what they do. They won't be on the job long enough to develop some mature toughness, or they'll become slack in their one common responsibility—safety and security.

Things were said and done to me that the average person would not have tolerated. The average school security officer would have just walked away from his duties or lost his cool (I discuss maintaining a cool head in Chapter Nine). These incidents just made me tougher. People can play with your mind, causing you to mentally beak down, resulting in a decline in your performance. Since the safety of students and staff is the primary focus of my job, staying mentally sharp is important. When I drive onto campus, it's important that I have a clear mind. I have to be able to think clearly, and carry out my thoughts in a professional and precise manner. When hundreds or thousands of children are involved, things can happen quickly. We must be mentally capable of maintaining issues within ourselves before we can resolve any external conflict effectively and successfully. The time to prepare ourselves mentally is not when all Hades breaks loose, but rather when things are quiet and calm.

In the course of performing my duties, I have to show mental toughness at two prime times each day: managing traffic in the morning, and again in the afternoon, when parents drop off and pick up their children. I was shocked to learn that so many parents did not obey the school's traffic rules. Many of them attempted to do whatever they desired. They were not concerned about the safety and security of all the students moving between and around cars and crossing the road to enter or leave the school. All they were concerned with was dropping off or picking up their child as close to the school building as possible and leaving campus as quickly as they could.

When parents refused to comply with my requests and directions, I had to stand tough and not back down. Parents got out of their cars to confront me while I was in the middle of conducting rush-hour traffic just to tell me how wrong and messed up I was. Parents took out their frustrations on me by cursing me and calling me names. The school even received complaints from parents about their displeasure with the way I conducted traffic. In each case, I had to be mentally tough and not lose my cool, because what I was doing was very important in maintaining the safety and security of the students, their own children included.

Many times during traffic duty a parent would take issue with me and with what I was doing and did not hesitate to let me know. Sometimes the conversation got somewhat heated. It's hard to be mentally tough in the middle of heated situations and still maintain control. But to me, that is exactly what mental toughness is all about. It's the ability to control your anger and temper when someone is displaying anger toward you. The duties you're attempting to carry out are vital to creating and maintaining safety and security. I could not allow these parents to deter me from my overall role—the safety of the children as they are dropped off, picked up, and while crossing the street as they entered and exited the school.

School security officers must keep themselves in top physical condition. As some people probably know, this is not a job where standing or sitting around is all that is necessary. Sometimes physical activity will be required. The body will follow the mind. The reason most people fail physically is because the body is not prepared to follow what they are thinking. Thinking with a clear mind is important, as is having the physical capacity to act on these thoughts. School security officers should at least be able to move from one place to another without becoming so exhausted that when they arrive, they cannot follow through on ending or minimizing a threat.

Conflicts don't always originate physically where you are. Many times, they start in places where you have to physically move to get to them. Moving from one room to another means putting your body into motion. Remember, students, staffs, and visitors are depending on you to keep them safe no matter where you or they happen to be in the school building or grounds. Getting there is a major part of your job. For instance, if you're working in a school that has an upstairs, and you happen to be downstairs when an incident occurs, it may be necessary for you to take the stairs rather than wasting time on the elevator.

I've learned that timing is important. The quicker I can get to a conflict, the quicker I can step in to try and defuse it. Your ability to arrive at a conflict, step in, and defuse it could determine whether a student or staff member gets harmed. The longer a verbal confrontation is allowed to continue, the greater the chance a physical confrontation will follow. I talk more about confrontations in Chapter Three.

I can tell you from personal experience that school security officers are required to be on their feet for long periods of time. This includes standing, walking, and sometimes running. These can also be made worst by extreme weather conditions, such as heat, cold, rain, and sometimes snow and ice. Just as we are required to maintain a certain standard of marksmanship skills and other qualifications, we should take it upon ourselves to maintain a certain standard of physical fitness for our bodies; doing so will greatly enhance our ability to get from point A to point B. Because of some of the situations that take place in our public schools today, physical toughness is vital for a school security officer. Remember: *If you don't make yourself visible, it's just like you're not there.* It is vitally important that school security officers get to the location where they're needed as quickly as they can, and then be able to intervene physically if necessary.

Physical toughness means *you* must be self-sustained. What I mean by self-sustained is, making sure you do the things necessary to take care of *you*. No one has to tell me to wear a raincoat when it's raining outside. No one has to tell me to wear a winter coat when it's cold outside. I don't want to take the focus off school security, which is what this book is about, but being in the security business may also provide you the opportunity to work other security jobs that are not school related. Some of these jobs, just like school security, can place demands on you that require mental and physical toughness.

One summer while school was not in session, I recall several school security officers, including myself, working voluntarily at an American Youth Soccer Organization event that the city was hosting. This huge event brought in children from all over the United States, even as far as California and Hawaii. The children ranged from nine to nineteen years old, and were accompanied by parents, grandparents, siblings, aunts, uncles, nieces, nephews, and friends. For six days we provided security at six different locations where soccer was being played. Each one of us worked a twelve-hour shift. My shift was from seven in the morning to seven in the evening. We all knew it would be a greater challenge with temperatures ranging from the mid-nineties to one hundred degrees or greater during the day and the early part of the evenings. And with the humidity, we had to be extra careful to keep ourselves hydrated and not get too hot while performing our duties. For me, it was a greater challenge just to drink enough water during my tour of duty, not to mention all the walking in the extreme heat in my uniform with all my gear. At my location I had five fields to cover, and they were not all in the same general location, so I had to do lots of walking.

Serving in the military taught me some things about being self-sustained. During my nearly twenty-five years of active duty service, I went on several deployments and field training exercises. Every deployment and training exercise required that we be self-sustained as a unit. Not only did it require us as a unit to be self-sustained, it also required each individual soldier to be self-sustained, with certain necessities needed for the duration of the event. Whether we moved as a brigade, battalion, company, platoon, or squad, moving self-sustained was important for soldiers' morale and the completion of the mission. Even though support elements may have been assigned to us, they were not designed to sustain us, only resupply us. Resupply is not the same as being self-sustain. Resupply means to replace what was once there, or replace new for old. Moving to a training exercise without the necessary supplies or equipment, depending on resupply, is a failed training exercise from the start, not to mention the low morale it would cause the soldiers. Careful thought and planning must go into the process of calculating just what supplies and equipment would be needed to complete the mission successfully, and maintain soldiers' safety and morale. If the unit is to accomplish these things, it must move with the necessary equipment and supplies needed to self-sustain itself for a period of time.

The period of time will depend on the mission, length of exercise, and the availability of resupply. Units cannot deploy with a one hundred percent guarantee that they'll be resupplied on a specific day and time. They must move with enough supplies and the right equipment to sustain them even past the scheduled resupply date. Each individual soldier must also move with enough individual supplies to maintain personal hygiene for an undetermined amount of time, as well as the proper and necessary issued clothing and equipment for proper uniform and safety. Personal hygiene supplies may be resupplied through purchase at the soldier's expense if facilities are available and time permits. The individual soldier usually maintains and controls issued clothing and equipment and these will not be resupplied under normal circumstances.

The message I want to get across to both school security officers and officers providing general security services is this: always be ready to face unpredictable conditions, and be prepared to perform in the midst of them. Be not only mentally prepared, but physically prepared also. I have the mentality that if I don't take care of *me*, it would be hard to help someone else if they needed my help. No one had to tell me it was going to be extremely hot and it was important to stay hydrated. I did not wait for someone to provide me water to drink or order me to pace myself. I came prepared to do what I was hired to do—provide safety and security.

Notes

Notes

CHAPTER TWO

A School Security Officer Must Be Firm

There are many professions where firmness is important in daily duties and responsibilities, and the job of a school security officer is one of those. In the course of a regular day, many questions will be asked of you, and you'll be expected to answer each of them, even if that answer is "I don't know." If you don't know, you're expected to find an answer that will hopefully be satisfying. Most of your answers will be based on information you know to be true or information you have received from a reliable source, such as a trusted co-worker, supervisor, or your headquarters. Just being on the job means students, staff, and parents look to you for answers on safety and security. Being firm in your answers in these situations may or may not mean you stand solid on your answers—we all know that information changes as situations change.

Remember, the safety and security of students, staff, parents, and visitors are your major responsibilities as a school security officer. If you know something is dangerous and allow it to take place, you're being irresponsible in your duties. These are times when firmness must be applied, without backing down. Some people won't necessarily agree with you, because it's not what they expected. Or they'll want to do something different. Being firm means you'll sometimes go against the will of others. But after all, it's your job to promote safety and security.

Your job will sometimes cause you to go against the will of students, staff, and parents. You're always thinking safety and security, while they might be thinking of other things. A dedicated school security officer must think with a different mindset, and see with a different set of eyes than everyone else at school. A dedicated and focused school security officer, in many cases, will foresee danger or possible problems before they happen. Because safety and security is the main focus, firmness is vital in this line of work. Standing firm in your decisions about safety and security will not be popular, but you're not on the job to gain popularity. If you know that your safety or the safety of others is at risk, stand firm in your decisions.

Most of my decisions and judgment calls are based on current or past information. Many times, my calls on safety and security decisions were made from past experiences, what I knew to be facts, or what I felt to be the best call. But even when things don't happen the way you had anticipated, you must still stand firm in your decisions about safety and security issues. This is no time to start second-guessing yourself. When it comes to the safety and security of children, it's best to err on the side of caution every time. Every time.

As a school security officer, there will undoubtedly be many times you have to make some hard calls related to the safety and security of those in your care. Many of those calls will not be favorable, and a few people will have trouble complying with them. Remember, they lack knowledge about why you made the call: Still, make your decision, and stand by it. After all, whatever the outcome is, you, as the officer, will be blamed. People will see you as the one in charge. And if things turn out badly, you'll be looked at as the "bad guy."

From my experience as a school security officer, once someone labels you as a bad guy, you're forever a bad guy in his or her eyes. When people label you as a bad guy, they'll often try to use their influence to convince others to see you as they see you. These people never stop to think why you had to be as firm as you were to get them to comply with your request. They never consider that safety and security were at the core of your actions. I've discovered that these types of people are dangerous, because they are usually *self*-focused. They don't care about anything but what matters to them at the time.

This is why they must be corrected and directed at the very first sign of self-focus. Every time I deal with people like this, I have to use firmness to establish and maintain safety and security.

No one wants to be known as the bad guy, but you might have to be the bad guy to establish and maintain safety and security. Sporting events are places where crowd control must be established and maintained. For you to accomplish this, firmness is your requests might be necessary, and this is when you become the bad guy. For example, you might have to tell people that no, they can't let their baby play on the field or floor during the game. Or no, they can't bring animals into the stadium, except for service animals. Then you must follow through by enforcing what you've requested.

I'm the so-called bad guy because I'm the one who has to look people in the eyes and tell them "no." I'm the bad guy when I have to correct small children who are running around creating an unsafe environment for themselves and others. Some people I've corrected have reacted in negative ways, and I always have to be prepared for that response. When people choose not to comply with my request even after the first, second, or third time, then I have to become the bad guy. Still, I always make it a point to be polite and ask in a respectful manner. My first request is always done in a calm manner and tone of voice. If I have to make a second request for the same issue, it's with a bit more authority. When I have to issue a third request, it's no longer a request, but an order. This is when firmness must be applied, even if it makes you the bad guy. School security officers are the bad guys because they have to use firmness to get someone to do what has been requested to establish and maintain safety and security. But remember, there will be times when the first request will have to be given with firmness because of safety or security reasons.

School sporting events are situations where I've had to exercise some of the most firmness in carrying out my duties and responsibilities. I can remember working many sporting events where I needed to use firmness to establish and maintain safety and security. One that comes to mind is a wrestling tournament for elementary and middle school students hosted by the school I was assigned to. The tournament had around fifteen hundred wrestlers in attendance that day. Of course, this brought out the parents, grandparents, uncles, aunts, cousins, siblings, and friends of those wrestlers. The event was held in the gym and atrium area. It started early in the morning, and lasted well into the night. My shift was from 6:00 am, until 2:00 p.m.

For safety and security reasons, only wrestlers, coaches, managers and trainers were allowed on the floor. Everyone else had to be off the floor and in the upper part of the gym. An announcement was made at the start of the event, and then several times throughout, informing everyone other than wrestlers, coaches, managers, and trainers that they *had to* be off the floor and in the upper seating area of the gym. Unfortunately, several parents and grandparents either did not hear the announcements or chose to ignore them because I had to tell several of them repeatedly that they were not allowed on the floor and that they must watch from upstairs. Amazingly, I had to tell the same people one, two, or even three times.

Because of these parents' and grandparents' negative behavior, I had to be firm to get and keep them off the floor. I was now the bad guy because I got firm with them. And because I was firm, some called me some pretty bad names. I even recall one woman saying I was prejudiced. Another woman looked me in the eyes and said, "I cannot be down here even if my child is about to wrestle?" I looked her in eyes and replied, "No," with a firm, authoritative voice. She turned away while murmuring words and returned upstairs. One would think that this would be the last time she would have to be told that she could not be on the floor, yet, once again she found her way back to the floor, this time bringing her husband with her. When I approached her this time, I started the conversation with, "Miss, if I have to tell you one more time to stay off the floor, I will ask you to leave the building." She looked at me as though she was confused about what I had said to her. She began to tell me how unfair I was and how I could look the other way if I really wanted to. As her husband stood there watching and listening to all of this, he took her by the arm and said, "Honey, be quiet. Let's go." As he was leading her away she was still running her mouth. Had I asked her to leave the building at that point, I would have been in the right.

I've come to learn that some people have a difficult time complying with parking rules. As a school security officer, part of my duties and responsibilities are making sure parking on campus is kept in check. Whether during normal school hours or sporting events, some people have a problem obeying the school policies on parking. It doesn't matter if a sign is posted stating "No parking" or security tape is strung that reads, "Caution, do not enter." Some people ignore these signs and proceed to park there anyway. When I attempt to explain to them why they can't park there or ask them to move their vehicle, I always get the question, "Why?" Then I proceed to explain why that particular area is off-limits to parking for them. After taking the time to do this, they still look at me with disbelief on their faces. Every time I get that look, I know it's time to be firm with any further requests.

I don't look forward to or enjoy these times. Many of these drivers are parents of students who attend the school where I work as school security. I desire to have a good relationship with all the parents, but some of them will not allow it because of their unwillingness to follow policies when it comes to parking and driving on campus. Now I have to be the bad guy once again to maintain safety and security. Outside sporting events that brought large crowds, such as football games, track-and-field, and cross-country, were times I had to use the most firmness related to parking on school campus.

I realize that not all school security officers have the same work ethic, but with willingness and hard work, this character trait can be learned and developed over time. I'm sure of one thing: if you're not comfortable with confronting, correcting, directing, and instructing people, you will not make a good school security officer, because these are part of the job requirements and are vital to creating and maintaining safety and security. Realize that not everyone is going to follow every school policy. Some will not follow policies simply because they don't know them, while others just choose not to follow them period. This is where you, the school security officer, have to step in and are forced to confront, correct, direct, or instruct those violating the rules to establish and maintain safety and security. With some students and parents, I've learned that confronting, correcting, directing, or instructing is not enough at times—this is when firmness is required. And don't be surprised if you have to repeat yourself with firmness before they begin to understand and comply with your request. This is not so much about getting them to do what you want them to do, but convincing them that safety and security are your top priorities.

Each time I have to use firmness, I make sure that I'm direct with my requests. I've learned from working around teenagers (and their parents) that you must be a "straight-shooter." What I mean by being a straight shooter is simple: tell them exactly what you want them to do. Don't hint at it be direct about it. By being a straight shooter with students and the people I come in contact with, I'm able to communicate to them exactly what I want them to do. Merely being firm will not necessarily get people's attention—you must also be a straight shooter. Two things will happen when being direct while using firmness. First, directness lets people know what your request is. Second, it allows them the opportunity to respond to your request. Still, even this doesn't work all the time.

Even though I enjoy what I do, I never enjoy the times when I have to be firm with students or adults. When firmness is necessary to establish and maintain safety and security, use your best judgment, and act with caution. Remember to be prepared to get tough and deal with situations the best you can while maintaining safety and security. And always be prepared to follow up your firmness with action if need be. As a school security officer, you must be ready and willing to inform people promptly what it is that you want them to do, and if they refuse to comply, then you must be willing to enforce your decision.

Notes

Notes

CHAPTER THREE

A School Security Officer Must Be Ready For Confrontations

I don't know of too many people who go around looking for confrontation. I would be willing to say the majority of people try to avoid confrontation at all cost. I suppose if you're a boxer, UFC fighter or wrestler, you can expect confrontation when face-to-face with an opponent; but these types of confrontations are conducted under rules and regulations to determine who is the greater of the two.

As a school security officer, you're sure to face some confrontational situations during your career. Even if you do everything to try to avoid them, they are bound to happen. Why do I say this? As I stated in the previous chapter, some people are not too keen on following directions and instructions. You'll come in contact with that student who just refuses to follow the school rules and will challenge you and your position as the school security officer. There will be times during the course of your duty day or at some sporting event that you'll become involved in a confrontation with a parent or some other grownup. Even though you do everything in your power beforehand to avoid it, it is inevitable.

The confrontational situations I've been involved in as a school security officer never came as a surprise. After dealing with children for a period of time, I learned to understand how some of them would react when confronted with authority. Some children became very defensive and rebelled at anything I wanted them to do. This is a recipe for confrontation. I would see it coming, and had to be ready to promptly deal with it. Likewise, certain parents seemed to have a chip on their shoulder, or for some reason thought they were above the law. Whenever these parents were around, and certain guidelines and rules had to be followed, I knew it was a strong possibility that at least one of them would defy the rules or school policy. Every time I had to approach one of these parents to correct, instruct, or assist, I was prepared for confrontation. Again, facing these parents who, for some reason or other have refused to follow the law of school policy is a recipe for confrontation.

Confrontation can take two different forms—verbal and physical altercation. Is one worse than the other? Well, you be the judge. Physical altercations can result immediately in bodily injuries, while verbal altercations can turn quickly into physical ones, which can result in bodily injuries. I've been involved in both, and I can tell you that there are no winners in either. They both put all parties at risk of something bad happening. That's why it's so important to get into and maintain control of all confrontations, whether verbal or physical. As I stated in the previous chapter, if you as a school security officer are afraid or just not comfortable with confronting people about safety and security at your school, then you'll not make a good school security officer. Confrontations must be dealt with at the first sign of them.

I had to step in and resolve many confrontations that started between other people or groups. As a school security officer, just because you don't have anything to do with what started the confrontation, you still have the responsibility of defusing it and restoring order. These types of confrontations can be more dangerous than the ones that surface involving you, because you don't know what you're walking into. It may not be clear if weapons are involved, or if you should concentrate on one person or group over the other. The focus instead is to separate the two as soon as possible. This will require some quick thinking on the part of the school security officer. The longer the confrontation is allowed to brew, the greater the possibility of someone being hurt. Just a word of caution when intervening in confrontations of this nature—proceed with care, but with a sense of urgency. You don't want to walk into something where you put yourself or your partner in any more danger. Another issue to consider when you get involved in these types of confrontations is: don't be surprised if you become the target of one or both parties.

Confrontations can happen anywhere, and at any time. Let me tell you a story of what happened to me after I was asked to intervene and assist with a student who was extremely disrespectful and noncompliant to the requests and demands of the administrative staff at the school where I worked. It was on a Monday afternoon around three thirty-five. I was conducting traffic when I received a call from one of the assistant principals requesting my assistance at the bus pickup. When I arrived, that assistant principal and one other were standing by one of the buses with the driver and a student. As I got closer, I noticed that the student was in the face of the bus driver and that they were exchanging words. After listening to the heated verbal altercation, I stepped in and told the bus driver we would handle it from here. At that time, both assistant principals instructed me to escort the student to the office and wait with him there.

The student and I made eye contact and I could sense from that point that I had my hands full. I quickly activated my body camera. The student immediately became resistant and very disrespectful, calling me names and telling me he was not going anywhere. I gently took hold of his left arm and continued to the office. On the way there I endured a barrage of verbal assaults. I asked the student several times for his name, but while he refused to tell me, he was quick to communicate what he thought of me. Once we arrived at the office, I asked him to have a seat but he refused, and continued his verbal assault on a nearby assistant principal and me.

This went on for some time. I saw the same look in his eyes I had seen when we made eye contact at the bus pickup. I requested again that he sit down but once again he refused. I finally got him to sit down, but not without some force. I quickly made an assessment of the situation and the danger this student was putting me and others in. Because other people were in the office area and with the inappropriate language he was using, I was asked to move him to the nearby conference room. I asked him to walk to the conference room, but he refused and continued to use vulgar language directed at the assistant principal and me. This student's violent demeanor and physical stance were creating an unsafe environment for everyone in the office area, and I was unsure what his next move would be. After he refused a number of requests to walk to the conference room, force was used to move him. He immediately began to resist, and assaulted me physically and verbally. He got in my face and pushed me backward. He grabbed my duty belt in an attempt to pull me to the floor. At that point, I made the decision to handcuff him, because he was trying to hurt me and could possibly gain control of some of my equipment.

After a physical altercation with him, I managed to get one hand cuffed and restrained him in a safe position until help arrived. When backup came, I was able to get his other hand cuffed. After he was secured in handcuffs and standing in an upright position, he then spat in my face. He was immediately restrained again. During the restraint, he began banging his head on a table, causing bleeding in the mouth area. An ambulance was called, as this was now about the child's safety.

Once emergency medical personal arrived, he would not respond to them and began to bang his head on the wall, floor, and his knees. When he did begin to respond, he told them he had not taken his meds for over a month and wanted to die. He stated that he had tried to kill himself.

This student was clearly suffering from an illness I had no knowledge of prior to my engagement with him. But does that mean I should have avoided the confrontation? No. It was within my scope of duties and responsibilities as the school security officer. When I intervened, he already had a short fuse, and I was not able to defuse it before the explosion. Other than having to receive a series of Hepatitis B shots, I was unhurt.

On that day I had not been expecting any type of confrontation, as I had only twenty-five minutes left of my duty. This is why a school security officer must always be ready for anything, at any time. Of all my confrontations with students and parents as a school security officer, this was one of my worst. A few days after the incident, someone asked me that if I found myself in a similar situation again, would I respond the same? My answer to them was yes, but with a qualifier. I explained I had never experienced two confrontations where everything was equal, and that I would have to assess each one and respond with the action I felt was appropriate at the time… but doing nothing was never an option. If it's a matter of safety and security—and all confrontations are—then something has to be done.

Sporting events are breeding grounds for confrontations. One night at one of the school's home basketball games, as two women started to walk in front of the cheerleaders to get to the other side of the gym; I approached them and asked them not to, but to walk around through the lobby because it could have created a safety hazard for them and the cheerleaders. After getting their attention, it was clear from their body language that they were going to challenge me. Once I was sure I had their attention, I began to make my request. I started the conversation with, "Excuse me, madam," followed by, "would you please…?" Neither of them was willing to do what I asked them to do.

It wasn't as if someone in street clothes had approached them and asked them to do something. I was in my duty uniform. Everyone could clearly see why I was there. Neither one of these women could have mistaken me for someone who had a duty other than safety and security. It was just pure disrespect on their part. It seemed as though they were looking for a confrontation. Both of these women had a few choice words for me, and continued to refuse to do what I asked them to do. They both continued to abuse me verbally and cause a commotion. I knew that if I allowed this behavior to continue, everyone in the gym would have been affected by their acts of disrespect. At this point, I ordered the older of the two to leave the building, which she refused to do, and the confrontation escalated. She had to be removed physically from the building.

To make a long story short, local authorities arrested the woman after she refused to obey all verbal orders given to her and started a verbal and physical exchange with them. This person turned out to be the mother of the other woman. I was shocked to learn that a mother had behaved this way in front of her daughter.

Notes

CHAPTER FOUR

A School Security Officer Must Be Fair

"Firm and fair" is the policy I use when dealing with children. Fairness is important when dealing with all people. Often, children don't understand the duties and responsibilities of a school security officer, and will sometimes question his or her actions. Still, it's important to treat all children equally. What you do to correct one is what you need to do for all. The way you respond to one group is the way you should respond to all groups. Treating one student or group of students differently from others in the same school is discriminatory. The job of the school security officer is not to discriminate, but to protect.

When fairness is absent, favoritism is present. Favoritism must be avoided when dealing with students. There will be a wide variety of students in all schools from all different backgrounds, cultures, and ethnicities, and with all different personalities. School security officers must not allow any one of these to affect their decision making. When corrections, directions, and teaching points are asserted toward one student over another, or one group over another, it must be done without showing favoritism.

I've always had a problem with students wearing headwear inside the school building. Not only does it look bad, but most importantly, it's also against school board policy. I also consider it to be a safety and security issue. For instance, students could hide drugs, weapons, or other contraband under it. One school I worked at I found pills in a student's hat. It can also be a way for gang members or so called "wanna-bees" to flash their colors. It doesn't matter who the student is or what GPA he or she has earned, or whether or not he or she plays sports; if I witness them with headwear on inside the building, I ask them to remove it. If school policy states, "Headwear is prohibited inside the school building," then all students should be held to that standard. Fairness is not demonstrated when a school security officer allows a "good" student to wear headwear in school while asking others to remove theirs. School security officers don't make the policies...we just help enforce them.

Students are very observant when another student is being corrected. Therefore, any on-the-spot corrections toward a student must be done without bias. Students will question leadership if they experience or see different reactions to other students for the same violation. Because school security officers are constantly in direct or indirect contact with students, fairness is important in correcting and directing them without predisposition in our instructions. These students are watching to see if the same treatment is applied for every student for the same incident. Even though some students will think or feel that they deserve special treatment, fairness toward all students is the best policy. Remember—the ultimate goal is not to make students happy, but to make wise decisions that will ensure their safety.

This is bound to happen: in whatever school you're privileged to serve, there will be at least one child attending that school that you know—maybe not closely, but perhaps you have a friendly relationship with his or her parents. They may attend the same church as you, or they are a long-time friend or family member. You may have watched their children grow from an infant to teenager, know where they live, and maybe have even visited each other's home from time to time. When these students have to be corrected or disciplined at your hands, fairness must be applied. There will come a time when you might have to face these students to correct or put things in order from a safety or security standpoint. Some of these students may expect you to ignore the safety or security violations they commit. Some may even think you should let them off the hook with no correction or discipline at all. It should not matter who the child's parents are or how long you have known them; fairness must be exercised in every situation. Even though these will likely be some of the most difficult times on your job, fairness is the best policy.

Favoritism shown toward students in an environment such as a school can lead to many negative actions. Some students will start to feel that they are in control and allowed to get away with anything, without any corrections or discipline. This can create a sense of insecurity among other students that could affect their learning abilities. Also, some students and staff will develop a sense of fear, knowing there's little or no correction or discipline applied to certain students who display negative behavior. Consequently, this could lead to non-reporting of safety and security concerns and negative behavior throughout the school, resulting in an unsafe environment. Furthermore, your reputation as the school security officer will be tarnished. You'll be perceived as one who doesn't care about the safety and security of the school and will be labeled as "incompetent" or "lazy." As a school security officer, your job is not to gain points with people or become their friend, but to keep students and staff safe and secure. I always approach my job with the mentality that says, "I would like for all people to like me, but if some don't because of my fair but firm approach to my duties and responsibilities, I would rather be known as the school security officer who keeps people safe than the one who is a friend with everyone."

Being fair may mean that you might have to show mercy in certain situations. School security officers must be able to assess a situation quickly and precisely to determine its safety and security risk. There will be times on your job when events and situations are not major safety and security issues. If the situation doesn't create or pose a safety and security concern, it may be an advantage to all parties involved that you show a little mercy and permit the activity to take place. This doesn't mean violating any laws or school policies, but evaluating every situation to determine whether or not it poses or could pose a major safety and security problem. Even if there are times when mercy is granted to allow or disallow any action, a safety and security risk assessment must be done. But because conditions can change quickly, we must be ready and willing to reverse our decision promptly if safety and security becomes an issue.

Notes

CHAPTER FIVE

A School Security Officer Must Be Consistent

How consistent are you in your job? Do you consistently go to work every day? Do you consistently arrive to work on time every day? Do you consistently try to do your very best each day? Are you consistently honest and true with your boss? Are you consistently honest and true to yourself? Are you consistently prompt in doing the things you're asked to do? What did your boss see in you the day he interviewed you for the job? Does he or she see the same qualities today? What was his or her first impression of you on your first day at work? Does he or she have the same impression about you today?

These are just a few questions we should ask ourselves to determine how consistent we are in our job. Consistency prepares us for that next promotion. Consistency says, "I'm a leader in the making." Leaders are self-made. Leaders will recognize there's a need, and then find ways to meet or fulfill that need. Your boss can't create or make a leader out of you unless you're willing to lead. Your boss can give you the opportunities to lead, but you must do the work to show him or her that you're ready for that position. Consistency is one of those things. When you're inconsistent in your job you're saying to your boss, "I'm not ready for the next step up. I'm not ready for promotion." But even if the promotion never happens, as a school security officer, consistency must be practiced.

Coming to work on time two or three days out of the week and being late the other days is a sure sign that you're not ready for a leadership position. Being a person of consistency is not only important in your job, but also in your home and where you worship. Consistency is important because it shows others that you care and you'll be there to serve them. Consistency proves that you're reliable and accountable. Consistency is a test to determine if you're worthy of more responsibility. In my opinion, the only thing worse than having a co-worker who is unreliable and unaccountable is a school security officer who is unreliable and cannot be depended on. I ask the question again: How consistent are you in your job? This is one question every school security officer must ask him or herself.

When we choose to be consistent about anything we do in life, willingness is the first thing that is required. After willingness, self-discipline must be developed. Without self-discipline, being consistent is virturally impossible. Willingness and self-discipline are what it will take for us to be the best at what we do. Self-discipline can be applied both postively and negatively to whatever we choose to be consistent about. For example, we can be self-disciplined when it comes to physical fitness, which is a positive, or we can be self-disciplined at making *excuses* when it comes to physical fitness. They both require self-discipline on the part of the person.

Consistency is important when enforcing safety and security rules inside the school, on school campuses, and with students and parents. What was an unsafe act yesterday will probably be an unsafe act today. School board policies don't usually change on a whim. When working with children, being consistent in your duties and responsibilities will determine how quickly and effectively you'll gain respect and accountability from them.

For instance, if you enforced the school policy of not wearing headwear inside the school building during school hours last week, and the policy has not changed, you need to continue to enforce the policy every day the policy is in effect. When students see that you're not consistent in enforcing the rules of the school, they'll begin to think that the violations they're committing aren't that important as they relate to school safety and security.

There are times when new students enroll after the school year has started. Many times, these students will come from out-of-state schools, or from schools where they were allowed to get away with certain violations. Making new students aware of the policies at their new school is important. Just because they're new to the school and its policies and procedures, they don't automatically receive a get-out-of-jail-free card when they violate them. They have to be told what the rules are and what is expected of them the first time a violation of school policy occurs. After that, when I witness them violating school policies, I have to be consistent in enforcing the policies by correcting the students, and if necessary, submitting a displinary write-up.

It has been my experience that students and teachers will come to you with safety and security concerns once you have proven to them that you're serious about your duties and responsibilities as the school security officer. But how you respond to them must be done with consistency. Students and teachers must know that when they come to you, you're going to follow up. When they see that you're consistent and prompt in your response to their concern, they'll develop a sense of consistency about reporting what they see, hear, or smell when they believe it to be a safety or security issue. Consequently, the whole school will become a safer place for all. I always let teachers know that they are my eyes, ears, and nose.

Every school security officer owes the assurance to our principals, students, and teachers that we are up to the task each and every day while on duty. Arriving at school each day with confidence, and then expressing that confidence through your actions, demonstrates that you're ready for whatever happens. You can't be very effective at your duties and responsibilities as a school security officer if you're up one day and down the next…it's not a job for a person with a "roller coaster" attitude. Remember, people are watching you and looking to you to keep them safe. To do this effectively, you must be a person who exercises and practices stability.

School security officers cannot allow themselves to be affected negatively by certain events. No principal will be happy with a school security officer who is shaken by every little change of events. As a school security officer, you must understand that your administrative staff will not always see things the way you do. Don't be easily taken off track when there's a disagreement between the two of you. If you approach the matter consistently with respect and professionalism, you'll come out a winner every time. Stability is a character trait that will be tested periodically. In the midst of trouble and confusion, those depending on you to provide safety and security want to be assured that they can count on you. As good school security officers, we will never allow ourselves to become complacent, even when we feel our efforts are not productive.

Principals, teachers, and students must see willingness and consistency in our work. Everyone must come to school each day with the feeling that they are safe while there. They must feel safe and know that you, the school security officer, are looking out for their safety and security today, just as you did yesterday and the day before, and will do the same tomorrow. Teachers perform better in the classroom when they know that they are safe while doing their job. Students and their parents are also relieved when they know that safety and security is consistently a high priority.

I'm reminded of how hard my parents worked to make a living. My parents worked on a farm until I was about nine or ten years old. My dad and mom were sharecroppers during the fifties and sixties. If there wasn't much profit from the crops during the year, then the boss didn't do much sharing at the end of the year. My dad's amount of crop yield would depend on the amount of profit gained that year. If it was a good crop year, the profit was good—at least we thought so. But he only got a small percentage of what was harvested each year. They didn't graduate from high school. They didn't attend college. But Mom and Dad were consistent at what they did. They were in the fields day after day. They kept food on the table, clothes on our backs, shoes on our feet, and a roof over our heads. It took hard work on the part of the whole family. My parents taught me about focusing on the points that were important in life. They taught me the importance of being consistent. They taught me the importance of being prompt in my duties and responsibilities. Here I am nearly fifty years later practicing this same quality—consistency.

Before you can be consistent on the job, you must first be consistent in showing up for work. Personally, I don't like to take days off from work. I guess I have my military background to thank for such regularity in going to work every day. I'm not suggesting that you should go to work if you're sick or have a family or other type of emergency, but having a headache or feeling tired doesn't qualify as an emergency. You must get into the habit of going to work every day and being on time. Being just five minutes late for work one day could result in a matter of life or death for the ones you're suppose to protect. I've discovered that if I intentionally practice being consistent in fulfilling my duties and responsibilities, I will eventually find myself being consistent at them without having to try.

Consistency will help you perform better in your job. It will help you be more alert and better prepared for whatever might happen, just as it did for me. This might sound a little crazy, but I actually look forward to going to work every day, even though some days are better than others. That is one thing I love about working as a school security officer—the mystery of not knowing what will happen from day to day, yet still being consistently ready for the unexpected.

Your goal as a school security officer should be to work consistently at your job as best you can. The people at your school where you serve are counting on you to report to work every day and be ready to do what you were hired to do—keep them safe and secure.

Notes

CHAPTER SIX

A School Security Officer Must be Alert at All Times While on Duty

School security officers must take their jobs seriously. Even if everyone else in the school goes about their day as though nothing bad can or will happen, you must stay alert to the situations around you. Just because nothing bad has happened yet doesn't mean it won't. School security officers can never adopt the mentality that nothing bad will happen where they are serving. Not being serious is a bad way to spend your day when you're responsible for the safety and security of the students and staff of an entire school. There should never be times when you're not mentally alert. Even if you have periods of time where you're allowed to rest your physical body, you should always remain mentally alert. School security officers must always operate with a positive skill set and mindset while on duty.

Knowing your surroundings and keeping a close watch on school security and safety can mean life or death for yourself or those entrusted to your care. Being alert and keeping a watchful eye on the people around you is imperative for the safety and security of those around you. With several hundred or thousand students to look after, alertness cannot be taken lightly. If I fail to be aware of what or who is around me and what is happening around me, I fail to keep students safe. I know that things happen outside of my control, but since my job is to control and manage things as they happen, I first must be aware of what is happening.

One way to be alert is by knowing the places where students congregate during class changes or where there are hundreds of students having lunch together. These places require special attention and alertness. Any areas where a large number of students gather with little or no other adult supervision are cause for attention on the part of school security officers. These areas all contain what I call "hot spots"—areas where a large group of students gather for the purpose of socializing or for some other, less-than-honorable purpose.

School sporting events are where I've had to be the most alert during my time as a school security officer. Every school sporting event has at least one hot spot. School sporting events are normally open to the public, and can draw people from a variety of surrounding neighborhoods and counties. Maintaining safety and security at some school sporting events is more of a challenge because they can have more than one hot spot; therefore posing a greater threat to school security officers. School sporting events are one place school security officers must be alert and ready to respond at a moment's notice. Some school sporting events can also present more of a security challenge than others because of the area to be secured. For example, outside sporting events are more challenging than those that are indoors, because it's much harder to maintain crowd control simply due to the amount of open space you have to deal with. Even if security tape or barriers are put in place, people don't always obey them.

It's easier to provide security and safety for indoor sporting events, such as basketball and volleyball games, and more formal events, such as graduation ceremonies, because everyone is contained in an enclosed area. But football games and other outdoor sporting events are different. For example, at football games, there could be hundreds or even thousands in attendance. Because there's so much space for students and adults to move about, security officers must watch their movements closely. If you're reading this book and have ever worked at a high school football game as a school security officer, then you know from experience that ninety percent of the young people who attend these games don't go there to watch the game. Generally, they tend to congregate in one or two specific areas creating a nightmare for school security officers. During these times, school security officers assigned to these areas must be focused and alert at all times. Most of the time we school security officers start out at a disadvantage—we are outnumbered. So, it's extremely important that we know what and who is around us, and that we be alert at all times.

Being alert at sporting events means not doing anything other than watching and observing those around you. This is not the time to be talking or texting on your phone. Cell phones can be distracting and dangerous for school security officers. I realize there are times when you must take a call from your spouse, child, or supervisor, but being on the phone for more than one or two minutes is dangerous because it distracts you from your duties and responsibilities. It's hazardous because you're not paying attention to your responsibilities—making sure those in your care are safe. Would-be troublemakers are going to be as aware of you as you are of them, and if you're distracted, that's when bad stuff is going to happen. It's impossible to text or talk on the phone while being alert and focused on your job. If you must take a call or read or send a text, be brief, then get back to business. Many are depending on your skills to help keep them safe and secure.

In addition, as basic as this may sound, school security officers are not at school sporting events to be a spectator. Nothing can divert you more quickly from your duties and responsibilities than watching the game. You might like all sports, you might like some sports, or you might not like any sports at all, but it doesn't matter: the energy and excitement around you will draw you in if you allow it.

Another distraction that can hinder alertness at sporting events and others places where your undivided attention is necessary is carrying on conversations with others, whether it's a student, parent, friend, family member, or another officer. I find it almost impossible to know what is going on around me when I'm engaged in a conversation. So, when I'm on duty, a lengthy conversation is just not going to happen. If I cannot talk to you without looking around, the conversation is over.

Most people don't understand the duties and responsibilities of a school security officer. Most of them just want to talk, not realizing the predicament they are putting you in. Most of them will talk until you end the conversation, which you may have to do. At the first sign a conversation with someone is going in the wrong direction, I apply the brakes. It's my job to find an easy out without being too disrespectful. Over time, I've learned who likes to talk at school sporting events. When I see these people I can either go in a different direction or simply smile and say, "Hello," or "Hi, how are you?" and keep moving. While most people understand that you have a job to do and will not feel you're trying to avoid them, others won't—they'll talk as long as you're willing to stand there and listen. This is why it's important for you to end a conversation quickly if it interferes with your duties and responsibilities of maintaining safety and security.

Throughout my eight years as a school security officer, I think I've had a good working relationship with the local law enforcement officers who were assigned to the school where I worked. But I cannot allow myself to be drawn into lengthy conversations that could distract me from my duties and responsibilities, whether I was working a football game or the school cafeteria during lunch. However, I've seen school security officers stand around and carry on lengthy conversations with local law enforcement personnel, and losing all focus on their primary duties. Not only does this look bad, it also sends the wrong message about what they were there to do. I made it a point not to allow myself to be caught up in conversations that were irrelevant to my duties and responsibilities. Yes, I would meet and greet, but that's just about as far I would allow the conversation to go.

Some might say that I was being anti-social by not engaging in long conversations with my fellow officers, but I was just being duty focused. I made a personal commitment to uphold safety and security to the best of my ability. There was no doubt I needed my fellow officers to help me maintain safety and security. Having the local law enforcement officers present, with their experience and special skills to tackle problems when they arose, was also comforting. But our duties and responsibilities are not the same in scope. When more than two officers stand around carrying on lengthy conversations, I call that "grouping." Grouping is a huge safety risk for both the officers and others, and puts them in potentially harmful positions. Grouping is a safety and security violation, and it appears unprofessional.

Often, family members distract school security officers from their duties and responsibilities at school events, especially children. This is something I've never understood: why would any school security officer, charged with providing safety and security at a school sporting event where there are hundreds or thousands of students and adults, put their own child in such danger? Are they really watching their child, or the crowd? They're putting not only their child in danger, but also themselves and their co-workers. If a fight or some other incident happened, would that officer be there for backup for his or her partner, or would they first protect their own child from danger? I know for myself that I would first protect my own child if trouble were to break out. I think officers who show up for duty at sporting events with their child are putting themselves in a position where they'll have to choose who they would protect if there was trouble. Also, having your spouse by your side is a huge safety risk. A spouse who understands the importance of safety and security will allow you to perform your duties and responsibilities without having to be by your side at such dangerous times.

Eating when one should be watching also diverts school security officers from being alert to their duties during sporting events and other places they have been assigned to conduct safety and security. I know that many school security officers may be offended by what I'm about to say, but it still needs to be said: it's very distracting, difficult, and unprofessional to be eating in front of hundreds or thousands of people when you're there to help keep them safe. If you must eat, I suggest you do it somewhere out of the public eye. But remember: *If you don't make yourself visible, it's just like you're not there.* You must decide what the higher priority is at the time. If you must eat, and there's another officer working with you, it would be wise to have that officer cover for you until you're finished eating. All these distractions can greatly affect the way you react, as well as your response time to a situation.

Drinking liquids like water and sport drinks are necessary during hot weather. But even when consuming these, keep your dominant hand free, stay focused and alert, and keep your guard up. Whenever possible, you should eat before you arrive for duty. There are exceptions, of course, such as medical reasons. Whenever I was scheduled to work security at a sporting event at a school I didn't normally work at, I found that most times, I had time to stop and get something to eat, or I brought extra food if I knew I was scheduled to work that night. I never waited until I was on duty to eat. If I'm on duty and doing something other than watching and observing the crowd, I'm being irresponsible. Even during the day at the school, eating before the lunches started was important. I would always snack in the mornings before the lunches started so that I would be available for security watch during school lunches. I knew I wouldn't have time to eat my lunch while the students ate. My job was to be present and alert in the cafeteria.

I've learned that the lunchroom is also a hot spot. This is a place where many verbal and physical altercations take place. This is a place where several students, sometimes hundreds, assemble for thirty minutes or more. This is a place where differences are settled between two students or two groups of students. Many times, they'll pick the lunchroom area to resolve ongoing disputes because this is the place where they'll have the largest audience and therefore, the most attention. This is the place where there are often no teachers to oversee and monitor their behavior. When you have this many children in one area, you must be alert.

During the time I've served as a school security officer, the lunchroom has always been a place where security is needed. It's vitally important for me to remain engaged in the students' activities when they're entering the lunchroom, during their time in lunchroom, and exiting the lunchroom. During those thirty minutes or more, I have to be alert, paying attention to what is happening around me. Once again, this is not a time to have my face buried in my cell phone, playing games, eating or texting. Nor is it a time when I'm engaged in conversation. If I get a call or need to make a call, I keep it brief and then I'm back to observing student behavior. This is not a time to be monitoring the hallways or the security cameras. My service is more valuable when I'm present in the lunchroom during that time of day. If I'm needed elsewhere, I am notified over the school radio that I carry with me.

Watching for students throwing food in the lunchroom is one of my priorities. Food fights in the lunchroom can get out of hand if not stopped at the very beginning. If you have ever been in the middle of a lunchroom food fight, you already know what I mean. Lunchroom food fights start with one or two students at one or more tables and can spread until every student at every table is involved in the fight. These are not pretty, and it can take a while to regain order. It's better to prevent a lunchroom food fight than to try to restore order once started. This is why being focused and engaged on what students are doing is so important. Being alert and keeping a watchful eye on the entire body of students is a good way to prevent a lunchroom food fight from starting or spreading. Remember: *If you don't make yourself visible, it's just like you're not there.*

When I work in the lunchroom, I walk around between the tables while the students are getting their food. After the majority of them are seated I continue walking, making sure each one of them sees me. I take a few steps, stop, and scan the entire room by turning my head and looking over the entire body of students. I repeat this process until I lay eyes on every student there. I continue this practice until all lunches are over. This is a chance for the students to see me as well.

I'm a big believer that if I'm visible to every student in the lunchroom, the ones who are looking to cause trouble will be deterred or, at least, delayed. My visibility also gives students the opportunity to report any safety concerns or issues they might have. Not only is the lunchroom a hot spot itself, but it also often contains different hot spots within it. Certain students pick a particular location within the lunchroom to sit to conduct their negative behavior. These locations require more visible presence than other locations in the lunchroom.

The lunchroom is one place where I've discovered that I'm not the only one doing the watching. The students, especially the more mischievous ones, are also watching me to see if I'm watching them. Before these students throw food or some other object, they look to see if I'm nearby. Many times, making eye contact is enough to deter or delay their negative behavior.

Being alert and aware of your surroundings is a skill that not only applies to school security officers, but to any job where you have to keep a watchful eye to maintain safety and security. I used to have a side job at a jewelry store as a security guard on top of my job as a school security officer. Because this business was open to the public, people of all kinds would come inside and shop. In my mind, I treated everyone who entered the store as a person who required me to be alert. I did not necessarily expect that everyone would try to steal something, but I still had to be alert and keep a watchful eye on their every move throughout the store. I could not allow myself to get too comfortable with people coming and going, even with those who were regulars.

In the same way, I never allow myself to get too comfortable at school sporting events where I know there will be hundreds or even thousands of children and adults in attendance. Each school sporting event is different from the one before. There will always be at least one person at each event who was not there at the last one—that one person changes the whole makeup of what you might have been used to. Staying alert is important to staying safe and alive.

Sporting events and other large school functions must be treated as places where trouble may happen. This is why it's important for school security officers to remain visible and be vigilant at all times to the entire crowd. I like to think that because of my presence and visibility to people in attendance at sporting events, many incidents that could have happened did not. Just as most children will act in a positive manner if they know their parents are watching, most people will think twice about doing something stupid or dangerous if they know a uniformed officer is *watching* them and not just standing around talking on his or her cell phone, carrying on a conversation with someone, or doing something else other than being vigilant. If you have your face buried in your cell phone, a whole lot can happen around you, and you'll never know about it until a fight breaks out. Even if you're visible to the students, you must be *alert*, watching them to maintain order and safety. Be vigilant! Remain vigilant!

Personally, I don't like to sit when I'm before a crowd of people. It portrays a bad image of the duties I'm there to perform. As the saying goes, "perception is everything." We can easily give people the wrong idea about who we are and what we stand for. If I'm sitting down and have to move quickly, it decreases my response time. I know that I'm more alert and in control when I am standing and moving about. If I'm sitting down I cannot move about from one place to another. As I said before, people are watching me just as much, or more, as I'm watching them. Being alert means I must be prompt, willing, and ready to respond at any given moment. *If you don't make yourself visible, it's just like you're not there.*

No matter what you think about anyone else's feelings or opinions about school security, as the school security officer, you must never become complacent about the safety and security of the school and the people you're charged to protect. Benjamin Franklin said, "He that's secure is not safe." School security officers must never come to a point where they consider all is well and secure. There's a long list of jobs where employees became complacent about their duties and responsibilities. When this happens they put themselves and those around them in danger and it could create a major safety and security risk. School security officers are at the top of that list. Be vigilant! Remain vigilant!

Notes

CHAPTER SEVEN

A School Security Officer Must Be Teachable and Ready to Teach

I've never had a course in criminal justice. The only training I've had in security is in the military and with my employer on the job. I've spent hundreds of hours pulling security during my military career, and I've also learned a lot in my eight years working as a school security officer. I learned some things from my security supervisors, my security training officer, co-workers, and by trial and error. But I would have to say that the students I'm hired to protect have taught me the most about my job. Not how to carry out my duties and responsibilities, but more what I could expect during the course of a regular school day. I've come to realize that even in my fifties; I can learn a whole lot from teenagers. Today's teenagers are different from the teenagers when I was young. When I was a teenager, we didn't have any of the electronic communication devices that teenagers have today, nor did we have any of the social media websites. In working with and around children, I've found that these can easily distract them from the more important things in life—listening to and following instructions related to their present and future success. Not to say that I or other teenagers during my time always listened and followed instruction, but we didn't have those items to distract us. Nowadays, many young people have to be instructed on the same issue several times over before they start to understand, while some never seem to get it.

Early on in my career, morning and afternoon traffic duty were times when I discovered that teaching and giving instructions became part of my duties as a school security officer. Even after several weeks of driving onto campus and going through the drop-off and pick-up lanes, some parents did not catch on as quickly as others. In addition, there were times when the parent dropping off or picking up his or her child was not familiar with the school's policy on traffic flow. Even though a copy of these policies had been sent to each child's home address, I had to be willing to stop all traffic to instruct those parents, grandparents, uncles, aunts, siblings, and friends on how traffic operated on my campus in order to maintain safety and security during these times. Regardless of whether or not they were familiar with the traffic flow, I had to remain firm in enforcing the school's policies and guidelines on traffic flow, because had I not, I would have been jeopardizing the safety and security of myself, students, and parents. I could not allow these people to make unsafe traffic movements that could have put my safety and the safety of all those in my care at risk.

Even though my job title doesn't contain the word "teacher," on numerous occasions I've had to teach certain students while remaining in the security mode. Many students have asked why they had to do something they were asked to do. Sometimes I chose to explain why it was important for them to comply with the requests of teachers, administrative staff, security, and other authority figures. And, there were other times when I did not give an explanation to their questions. Many students simply don't know the school policies concerning the violations they're committing, but some know and just don't care. Whatever the case, if I feel it necessary and time permits, I try to instruct the student on what is right, explain why it has to be that way, and list the consequences they could face if they don't comply. I find myself instructing students on safety and security issues every day. Most of these students are only one-time offenders after I have a brief instructing session with them. This approach helps me build a better relationship with the students simply because they realize I care about their safety and the safety of the whole school.

Often when I teach, instruct, or direct, it requires me to be in the spotlight. I personally don't like being the subject of attention, but find myself in that position frequently when I'm required to give instructions or directions. I learned quickly that being in the spotlight was a major part of my job. Just because I didn't like it, that didn't mean it wasn't going to happen. My job required it at times, so if doing my job meant I would be in the spotlight, then so be it. Being in the spotlight means you're looked upon as if no one else is around and you become the center of attention. People's eyes will gravitate automatically toward you whenever and wherever you approach an individual or a group of people to offer any type of assistance.

Bandanas are unauthorized for headwear and any public display in the public schools where I work. As a school security officer, I have to confront students who wear them. There are times when certain students wear them as a way to signify their gang affiliation. In the gang world, it's called "flashing colors." Other students wear bandanas, mainly females, as a fashion accessory and have no clue that they could be putting themselves in danger based on the color of the bandana and what it represents in the eyes of some others. Whenever I approach a student for wearing a bandana, I make sure he or she understands that bandanas are not allowed to be worn in school, what the bandana could represent, and how it could be offensive to those who associate themselves with a particular gang. In an environment like a school, teaching along these lines is important, because most students are unaware of the unrest a bandana of a certain color could cause.

School security officers are already in the spotlight simply because they stand out from others in their surroundings. Just the uniform alone brings attention to us. Many times, this attention is elevated by others who refuse to comply with school safety and security rules. Anytime school security officers have to confront someone to teach, instruct, or direct, it brings unwanted attention to them. It's important that school security officers are aware that a spotlight is placed on us every time we step amongst a crowd for any reason. Being in the spotlight is something you'll have to get used to, because it will happen on almost a daily basis.

When it comes to teaching, instructing, or directing, you must be ready and willing to do this with all people you come in contact with. I discovered that it was not just students or parents that needed correcting, but even small children and grandparents. Many parents would bring their small children to sporting events and then leave them to take care of themselves. You'd be surprised at the things some of these children could get into. The average school security officer takes the position that these children are not their responsibility, and that they can do as they please. A *good* school security officer will not take this position. A good school security officer will be thinking of the safety and security of the child, and will do whatever is necessary to establish and maintain it. Sometimes it might require correcting and instructing coupled with directing. The school security officer must be ready and willing to do whatever is required, within reasons and lawfully, to establish and maintain safety and security for everyone.

There have been times when I was charged with instructing, directing, or correcting people of high official positions or ranks. A good school security officer will have no problem approaching these people, if required. Just because they are VIPs, they don't get a free pass to violate safety and security rules. Nor are you allowed to permit them to perform unsafe acts just because they hold high official positions. It doesn't matter if the person is old, young, male, or female; if you observe a safety or security matter or feel it's necessary to direct or correct someone, it must be done in a prompt, fair, consistent, and professional manner.

I learned to understand that when I fail to teach, instruct, and direct, not only do I fail to do my job properly, but I also fail at establishing and maintaining safety and security for the people and places I'm entrusted with. On the other hand, I have to remain teachable to learn from my mistakes and the situations I'm involved in on a daily basis. If I had maintained a daily journal of all the issues that came up from day to day, I would be able to go back to see that I learned at least one new thing each day on the job. I've used each of these issues to teach *myself* something, which helped me become a better school security officer. Every day is a learning experience for me. Because I wanted to learn all I could about being a school security officer, I took on security jobs where events were held in the school, but not sponsored by the school. I didn't take these jobs because I needed the money, even though the money came in handy, but rather I wanted the experience. I wanted to see what it was like to operate in different environments. I learned that no two events are the same. Each one has something different about it. I used these differences to teach myself about doing security in different environments where the administrative procedures are different, and a different set of rules applied. I viewed every security job as an educational experience, because they all were unique in some way.

I also learned to understand that it was important to take seriously the teaching and training we receive as a group. Being on time and paying attention to instructions and teaching, whether by an individual or videos, are valuable ways I received knowledge and understanding. Failure to arrive to training on time, or not being attentive during instruction times, could cause me to miss the very information I needed to save my life or the lives of others. In the military, I took all my training seriously, because I never knew when I might be called upon to put my training into action. I was taught to "train as I would fight."

Tasks not related to my duties and responsibilities as a school security officer taught me some valuable lessons as well. Some people will frown at the thought of performing tasks not within their so-called "duty description." I've learned to embrace every task as a learning experience. Whether or not it was a task within my duty description, I always took each one as an opportunity to expand my knowledge or gain new knowledge about a particular thing or new way of doing it. When I joined the military, I chose a Military Occupational Skill in the automotive area. I will tell you that not a day went by when I didn't perform tasks that were not related to my MOS, and because of that, I became a better soldier. Every job that I've had came with additional tasks. Because I chose to accept them as a learning experience, I'm a better person because of it. I strongly believe it's the reason for my aggressive work ethics.

As a school security officer, you might, and probably will at some point, be asked to do certain tasks you feel are not anywhere close to your duties and responsibilities. When this happens, don't reject the opportunity to teach yourself something different, or gain additional knowledge about something you have already been exposed to. Learn to accept every task as a learning experience. Your goal as a school security officer should be to be the best school security officer you can possibly be, so don't dismiss tasks that are not tied directly to your duties. This way, you'll always be learning and widening your chances for a more successful career. There may come a day when you no longer desire to be in the security business, and you'll move on to another job. Your next job might require some of the same tasks you rejected or frowned upon as a school security officer. A willingness to be teachable is not a sign of weakness or gullibility.

Notes

Notes

CHAPTER EIGHT

A School Security Officer Must Know His or Her Boundaries

Every school security officer must know his or her boundaries when dealing with students and staff. There are boundaries in every relationship, whatever level it's on. From the very first day on the job, there must be a separation between responsibility and relationship. This separation is something the school security officer must initiate. People will attempt to get close to you by trying to develop a friendly relationship with you. Most of these people don't have an ulterior motive for wanting to be friendly with you—they simply desire to know their school security officer. They want to be able to come to you if they need to without feeling like a stranger or that they're being bothersome. I've served at two different high schools as a school security officer. At both schools, I established a very good working relationship with most of the staff. I desired this type of relationship because I realized quickly that I could not carry out my duties and responsibilities effectively without the full cooperation and support of the staff.

Counselors, teachers, custodians, and food service personnel are valuable sources for information about students and for what is happening around the school. I would always remind teachers and counselors that they were my eyes, ears, and nose, and that I could not do my job effectively without their help. Nevertheless, I had to maintain boundaries, separating my duty from relationships with them. I worked to establish and maintain a relationship that allowed staff members the freedom and comfort to provide me with important information related to security and safety.

I'm always very careful about sharing information with teachers about students; it's always on a strictly need-to-know basis. Some information about students I did not share with anyone other than the administrative staff. It may not have been confidential or secret, but I wanted to maintain that trust and relationship I developed with them. Additionally, I made it a point to stay out of a teachers' business unless they invited me in. I allowed teachers to deal with their own classroom behavior issues. I'm a big believer that teachers are the best ones to maintain order in their classroom.

At my last school, I had what I would consider a wonderful working relationship with my administrative staff. We joked, laughed, and sometimes cried together. We could talk about nearly anything. We all worked very closely together to maintain school safety and security. But even in such close relationships, I knew where my boundary lines were. I kept my relationship with them solely professional, to the point that there was never a question in my mind or theirs of what my duties and responsibilities entailed. When it was time to get down to business, no one wondered whether or not I was serious, or capable of doing my job at that appointed time. Many days, our relationships went from kidding around one minute to the serious business of caring for significant school safety in the next minute. I learned to put up and take down boundary walls between duty and relationships appropriately, a skill that was vital in my duties.

The schools at which I've worked normally have a table in the lunchroom where the principals sit during school lunches. Every day, at least one or two administrators are present. Even though I have a good working relationship with them all, I don't hang out at their table. But even though I stay out of their business, it doesn't mean that they must stay out of my business—my business *is* their business. The quicker school security officers acknowledge and learn to live with this, the better their days will go as they work to develop and maintain that working relationship with administrators. Because of the working relationship I cultivated with my administrators, we shared information about certain students when it was warranted. I, however, did not share information about students when it was out of my range of duties and responsibilities, and I never expected them to, either. These were boundary lines I was not willing to cross.

I worked hard to create, develop, and maintain good working relationships with the principals. It was not something I felt was their prerogative; it was my responsibility to work hard to gain such a relationship if I desired their support related to the safety and security of the school. When things didn't go the way I thought they should have or the way I desired them to, I didn't make excuses or show frustration, but learned to have a reality check with myself. I am not in charge of the school. The head principal and his or her vice-principals are in charge. I am to support them in maintaining the safety and security of the school. It is my responsibility to gain their respect and trust. I have to prove to them by my actions and, in some cases, words, that I care about my duties and responsibilities and that I am there to do the best job I can possibly do. Establishing trust in an environment like a school can take some time, and will depend on each individual's work ethic. My work ethic regarding the safety and security of the school is a major reason for my positive working relationship with my principals. I learned that the more I proved to students and staff members how much I cared about their safety, the more trust I gained from them. Like John Maxwell said, "People don't care how much you know, until they know how much you care."

Boundary lines between your relationship with your principals and your duties as a school security officer must be kept separate. Don't attempt to speak your opinion on every subject that comes up. I learned to speak when spoken to and answer when asked a question. This attitude goes a long way with principals. If you're good at what you do, let it show through your actions, and not words only. We can all prove our work ethic through our actions while being silent. Principals are glad to have you there, but you have to earn your place with them.

Earning your position will also depend on how you show your respect toward them. There must be boundary lines set by you, the school security officer, when it comes to respect and honor if you want to have their full support in doing your job. It would have done me no good to disrespect and dishonor the school principals and then expect to have their full backing when it came to safety and security issues. If I want the support and respect of the administrative staff in doing my job, it's important for me to show respect and honor toward their positions. This is not something I have to do sometimes, but at all times. I do not choose to respect and honor them only when I get my way; rather I show respect and honor whether or not we agree on everything. This is hard for some people to do.

From my experience, most of the times when employees feel like their employer is not supporting them, there's a feeling of disrespect and dishonor on the part of the employee. Remember, it's your responsibility as school security officers to establish and maintain trust and respect between you and the administrative staff. This might not be an easy thing to do at the beginning, but if you work at it, the relationship between you and your principals will develop over time. Once you realize mutual respect and honor are being practiced, do everything in your power to keep them. I cannot stress this enough: it's not the sole responsibility of your principals to make the relationship a positive one. At times it may seem like they're doing things to sabotage the relationship. Remember, they are principals of the entire school body. They have to deal with unhappy parents from time to time. They have a lot on their plate! I learned that having things go my way all the time was not worth damaging the relationship I had worked so hard to establish and maintain.

Many students will also try to become friendly with you. Keeping boundaries here is vitally important. I learned that some students just want to know you because of what you do and are curious about your job, while others use this tactic as an opportunity to violate school rules and policies. I came to learn when students were genuine in their interest in what I did versus having an ulterior motive for their interest. But even with those who appeared to be genuine, it was my responsibility to maintain the boundary lines between duty and relationship. Whenever a student says to me, "You're my friend," I correct him or her on the spot. I say, "I'm not your friend, but I will be friendly as much as you allow me to be." By letting them know this, I draw a boundary line between duty and relationship. I cannot let them think that they have a privileged relationship with me that other students don't have. Don't get me wrong; there have been students who simply presented themselves as being the friendly type and would offer me a high five, fist bump, or handshake. I even make these students aware that there are boundaries in our relationship that separate duty and friendship. It's always important for me not to allow students to think or feel that they could cross those boundary lines.

There are many reasons for this, but safety and security are the main reasons, because they are my consistent focus. Make your boundary lines clear so that students, staff, parents, and everyone you come in contact with while on duty will know just how far you'll allow them to go before you have to enforce those boundary lines. As good school security officers, we must conduct ourselves so that people will come to know what boundaries *not* to cross with you.

Finally, you need to know how far to go with the power you may have been granted. As a school security officer, you have been given certain duties and responsibilities. You must be careful not to violate the power you have been given by your supervisor, principals, and the school board. As I mentioned in my introduction, the duties and responsibilities of a school security officer and those of law enforcement personnel are different in scope, and you must be very careful not to allow your actions on the job to mirror those of the law enforcement officer assigned to the school. I've witnessed, more than once, instances where a school security officer gradually diverts from his or her primary duties and responsibilities and takes on those of the law enforcement officer assigned to the school. For example, when school security officers have the duty and responsibility of watching those in attendance at sporting events, they cannot be standing alongside law enforcement officers engaged in *long* conversations. Law enforcement officers are usually at these sporting events to offer a show of support and force from the local law authority. They are not required to watch and observe as school security officers are.

Local law enforcement officers are more observed *by* the people than observers *of* the people—not so with school security officers. They are both observed by the people *and* observers of the people. When school security officers start to act and do as law enforcement officers, they violate the power they have been granted, and could put themselves and others in great danger.

School policies and procedures provide dividing lines between the two. Both parties must respect these lines to establish and maintain a healthy work environment and relationship. Whether it's at a sporting event or while on cafeteria duty, school security officers must stay in their lane of operation. We are *not* the police—we are school security officers! It will do every school security officer well to understand this. It doesn't matter if you have prior training in law enforcement; you're still not the law. Rather, use your training to become a good school security officer, and work to be a better one.

Notes

Notes

CHAPTER NINE

A School Security Officer Must Be Able to Function Effectively Under Pressure

Being in control of *yourself* at all times is vital for functioning effectively under pressure or in difficult situations. As I mentioned in Chapter One, when I drive onto campus every morning, I prepare myself for whatever might happen. I don't know and cannot predict what that day or any other day, will be like. It could start off just fine, but end in total disaster. Or, things could go south the second I arrive on campus and remain that way for the entire day. On the other hand, the whole day could proceed without any trouble at all. All it takes is one person or one incident to take things from good to bad, and you must be ready to meet difficulties head on. Whatever situation you might find yourself in, you must be effective in dealing with it. People are looking to you to defuse problematic situations and restore order.

A good school security officer will rehearse in his or her mind every day how they would react if a catastrophic situation developed at their school. Each day as I walk the hallways, I play out in my mind what my course of action would be if different situations were to happen. I don't rehearse these situations because I expect or have even heard of a potential threat, but because I want to be mindful and prepared if something were to happen. Pressure can present itself so quickly that many times, we don't even have time to think. Even when you're in training, pressure can overtake your mind, therefore overtaking *you* and the situation. If pressure can do this in training, just imagine the effect pressure can have on real-life events. You and I cannot control the actions of others or the messes created by the actions of others, but we can control how we react to them. School security officers must be able to operate effectively under pressure— and sometimes *extreme* pressure—to take control of a troublesome situation and restore order.

Inside the school is not the only place I run scenarios in my head. Sporting events, special school functions, and traffic duty are also times and places where the possibility of trouble could turn up. These places are the most difficult to maintain safety and security. Having a plan of action if trouble breaks out is important for your survival and winning. I make sure I know where entries and exits are located and the quickest way to them from wherever I am located. I do this every time I go to a restaurant or theatre. Preparation is the key to survival sometimes. Making myself knowledgeable of this information takes a lot of pressure off myself. When I don't know my surroundings, I feel boxed in. Being surrounded by hundreds or thousands of people can put anyone under pressure. I can't allow myself to be under such immense pressure that it takes away my ability to perform my duties as school security officer. As I mentioned before, sporting events are places with hot spots and we (school security officers) are outnumbered. Even thinking about how I would react to trouble if it were to break out is enough pressure by itself.

Parents can put pressure on you too, especially during sporting events. I've had to speak with parents who felt that simply because their child was participating in the event that day, they should have the liberty to do and go wherever and whenever they pleased. I've had to teach, instruct, and direct these parents. Most of them didn't like what I had to say, but my word choices have always been based on the safety and security of the whole event.

One way I discovered to minimize pressure from overpowering me was to learn the layout of the area I was charged with securing. This is critical in minimizing or defusing trouble or threats. I start with the interior of the school building, because that's where I spend most of my day. If you have to respond to a certain location in your school building, how fast you get there could mean life or death for a student or staff member. Knowing the quickest and fastest way to that trouble spot depends on your knowledge of the layout of the interior of the building. Every school I've ever worked at had a different interior layout, and it was imperative for me to teach myself how to get around inside them. I needed to be able to go from one area to another in the shortest possible time without losing my way. This required me to walk the entire interior layout of the school building several times each day until I was comfortable enough to get around without having to ask for directions. Just as I find it important to know my way around in my own house, it's just as important that I know my way around whatever school I'm working at. We become so comfortable in our own homes that we can even find our way around in the dark, and it takes the pressure off should we ever have to escape or move quickly from one room to another. In the same way, good school security officers should know how to get around inside their schools, even when lighting is no longer available. If you ever have to go from one area to another in the dark, being familiar with the layout of your school will take a whole lot of pressure off you.

Learning to use the building camera system is another way that I take some of the pressure off myself. If you're fortunate enough to work in a school equipped with cameras, learn to use them, learn where they are located, and learn their coverage area. It would also be helpful to learn where the "dead spots" are. These are spots where there's no camera coverage. I've learned that certain students study the location of the cameras in my school and the direction they are pointed. They also study and know where the dead spots are. A good school security officer will always desire more cameras to cover dead spots, but if they never materialize, it will not deter us from maximizing the use of the ones already installed.

While I walk the interior of the building, I observe where cameras are placed and the direction in which they are pointing. I've found cameras to be great tools in assisting me to do my job. When I started working at a new school, I took several days during the first few months to teach myself where each camera was located in each of the hallways. Because I didn't want the students to be aware of what I was doing, I would show up for work early and walk the hallways, looking at each camera in the hallways and stairways throughout the building. I continued this until I knew where each camera was located and the direction it was pointing. I also did this for the exterior cameras. Both interior and exterior cameras have helped me perform my job of maintaining the safety and security of the school more effectively.

As a school security officer, you're going to be confronted with some issues that will put pressure on you, but you cannot allow the pressure of the situation impede your effectiveness. Each day will be different. Every person deals with pressure in his or her own way. The ultimate goal is to deal with it while still performing your duties and responsibilities effectively.

Notes

Notes

CHAPTER TEN

A School Security Officer Must <u>Not</u> Be Schedule-Driven

Every one of us has certain things that we choose to do the same way at the same time each day. I get up five days a week (Monday thru Friday) and hit the gym for my morning workout. After my workout, I shave and shower, go back home, eat my ritual high-protein, high carbrohydrate-breakfast, get dressed for work, and leave at the same time each morning to arrive at school before children start to show up. I would repeat these behaviors ninety-nine precent of the time every week during the nine-month school year. Do you see a pattern here? We all have a little Obsessive Compulsive Disorder in us. Having a pattern in the way we get thing done on a daily basis is not bad in itself. But, in certain high-profile occupations, having a set pattern of how things must be done and when they are done can be costly. A school security officer is one of them. Granted, there may be certain tasks and duties that must be done at a set time every day, but we should not get too comfortable with them.

I'm responsibile for doing certain tasks consistently each day. As important as these tasks are, I've never allowed them to put me into an schedule-focused routine. I had to develop the mindset and mentality that every day would be different. It's easy for us to become accustomed to a pattern of doing things. As a school security officer, I've learned that I have to be ready and willing to adjust and rearrange some of the tasks I perform daily. When we becomes schedule oriented, we lose focus of other situations that could happen around us. When we become so focused on running our routines, we fail to prepare mentally for the unexpected. Even though we can never prepare ourselves fully for everything that could possibly happen, we must go about our daily duties and responsibilities with the mindset that something might happen that could take us away from our daily schedule. And believe me, in my experience, when you have the responsibility for several hundred or a few thousand children, the unexpected is bound to happen.

Let me give you an example. At one of the schools I worked at, one of the daily tasks I performed was directing morning and afternoon traffic in front of the school. This task was important, because this was where students crossed the road while going to and from the school. It was also the place where students were dropped off and picked up by their parents or other family members. So, with hundreds of students crossing in the morning and the afternoon, and a hundred or more cars dropping students off, there were always concerns for the safety and security of the students as well as the drivers. I always tried to be there to conduct traffic and help students cross the road safely. But if the principal asked me to be somewhere else during that time, I could easily make the transistion and adjust. Not being schedule-driven meant I was able to divert myself from the traffic-duty mindset to attend to a different task that required my presence. I did not have a "set-in-stone" schedule. In others words, I didn't allow myself to become schedule focused, but rather maintained my focus on safety and security. This is vitally important, because in a public school environment, things can change for the worse as quickly as you can take your next breath.

Schedule-driven school security officers can put themselves, not to mention others, in more danger than they already are. It's a bad habit to be at the same place at the same time each and every day. When this happens, people start to know of your whereabouts at certain times of the day. This is a major security risk inside schools. I'm very conscientious about where I choose to be during class changes. I always try to be somewhere near a hot spot, but never the same place each day. Remember, certain students are watching you and your patterns of behavior intentionally. From the time school is in session until it's out, I've always tried to have students wondering where I would show up next. Not being schedule-driven will allow you to make changes and adjust where you or your principals feel you need to be.

Schedule-driven people have a hard time dealing with change. There will surely be changes in your normal daily activities on occasion. Most of the time, we have no control over how the change takes place, or the effect it will have on the rest of our daily duties and responsibilities. But when we allow flexibility in our schedule, we are mentally prepared and better able to deal with it when it happens. And when change comes (not *if* it comes—*when* it comes), the quicker you embrace it, the quicker you can start to move forward in doing whatever you need to do to come out as the victor instead of being a victim. Remember, you might only have a few minutes or even seconds to make a decision. Even if it turns out not to be the right decision, make it and then move into action to take control of the situation. Standing around doing nothing will result in nothing being done. Learn to embrace change—don't go about your day as an schedule-driven school security officer. Otherwise, you will not know how to deal with change when it inevitably comes.

There may come a time when you're reassigned to a different school. Whether this reassignment comes at the beginning of the school year or in the middle, you must be willing, prompt, and ready to make that move. Schedule-driven school security officers will have a difficult time making the transition from a school that they are familiar with to a school that they might not know anything about. School security officers should never get too comfortable at their current school.

The military taught me flexibility. I've learned to be flexible in every job I've done. School security officers should not be schedule-driven to the point where they lose self-control when the news comes that they are being reassigned to a different school. If you're reassigned, your responsibility as the new school security officer is to learn all you can about the school's layout, the surrounding community, and the student body as quickly as possible.

The only thing we as school security officers should be driven by is our desire to keep students safe while they are under our care. This should be the driving force behind why we come to work every day and do what we do.

Notes

Notes

CHAPTER ELEVEN

A School Security Officer Must Be Professional About His or Her Duties and Responsibilities

Wherever we choose to be employed and whatever job we choose to do, we must be willing to follow certain protocols to establish and maintain a healthy, productive working relationship with our boss and co-workers. If, for whatever reason, we cannot show respect to those in superior positions, we'll have a difficult time at our job. You might know your duties and responsibilities as well as you know your name, but if you go about them without showing respect and honor toward your boss, you're not a professional at your job in his or her eyes, and will be viewed as a failure. Being professional toward your supervisor(s) is one way of showing them that you aim to be professional at your job. Your place of duty is not a place for you to wear your feelings on your sleeve. Chances are your feelings will be hurt at some point while you're performing your duties and responsibilities as a school security officer. The question is, how are you going to react to it? Professionalism cannot take a back seat to hurt feelings.

A good school security officer must also work to be respected for being professional. To be successful at our duties and responsibilities, a good school security officer must have the respect of those we serve. This is not to say that everyone will respect you as a person or for what you do. Still, it's important to gain and maintain the respect of the ones you're assigned to protect. I will be the first to tell you that this will not always be the case at your school. I've never had a problem with the administration, staff, or teachers respecting me at the school where I worked. It was mainly certain students who failed to show respect. I will be the first to admit that I've said things that, after I said them, I wished I had not. Also, I've handled certain situations in such a way that when I look backed, I wish I had handled them differently.

Working as a school security officer, I discovered quickly that children could act in such a way that reminded me that the "old man" in me is very much still alive. But, even in these times I had to be as professional as I knew how to be. However, I've learned that it's more important to have the respect of my administrators and their staff members than that of the students. Do I want the students to respect me? Certainly! Do they all show respect toward me? Of course not! This is something I quickly came to accept as part of my job: some would not respect my job or me. But that didn't change my professionalism during my job or toward my superiors. Having the respect of every student at my school doesn't have priority over professionalism. Having the respect of the principals, staff, and students means they view me as being professional at my job. Having their respect also means I have their support.

Professionalism requires a certain level of loyalty toward your employer, immediate supervisor(s), and your co-workers. Loyalty is another characteristic that has been lost between employer and employee. But remember: showing loyalty toward your principal(s) is one of the most important characteristics you can have. It's nice if the loyalty travels both ways, but even if you feel that your principal(s) doesn't have a sense of loyalty toward you, it's still your responsibility to show him or her loyalty. This will be more of a challenge when you have more than one principal to answer to. In this case, my advice is to be honest and true, which you should always be, and they will see your loyalty. People will see you for who you are. If you present yourself as a professional at what you do, the chances of you being perceived as one are very likely. Likewise, if you present yourself as being unprofessional, people will have the perception that you're unprofessional at your work.

Someone once said, "I don't have a problem with authority, I just have a problem with someone telling me what to do." People who think and feel this way not only have a problem with someone telling them what to do, but they also have a problem with life. Failing to follow instructions and not doing what you were hired to do is unprofessional. Most of our lives are lived with someone telling us what to do and what not to do. In the society we live in, a form of leadership is everywhere we look. There's leadership in the church, in the schools, in the market places, in the prisons, in the home, and on your job. Whoever your leader or boss happens to be, remember you didn't put him there, and chances are you won't succeed in removing him. If there's leadership you just cannot deal with on your job, then it may be time for you to find other employment. But don't be surprised if, when you get to your next job, there will be someone there telling you what to do.

There will always be someone higher up the chain than you. Your boss has a boss. Your boss boss has a boss. Their leadership may not be close by, but you are expected to obey it even if it's a thousand miles away. I can tell you a thing or two about obeying leadership. I spent nearly twenty-five years, in the military and during that time, not one day went by without someone giving me orders to do something or not do something. Oh yes, I gave orders too, but I had to obey the orders and commands issued to me. It goes both ways. It seemed like the more rank I earned, the more orders were given to me and the more I gave. Every good leader was an obedient follower at some time. Before anyone can become a good leader, they must prove to be a good follower, which is professionalism at its purest.

I think some people are under the impression that they have to like their boss before they are required to do their job. It would help if you and your boss did get along well on the job. But if you and your boss don't see eye-to-eye, you're still expected to do your job with a high level of professionalism. Your boss did not force you to take that job. Be thankful for your job, your employer, your co-workers, and your boss. It may not be the place that you plan to stay for the rest of your life, but that is where you are right now. If you cannot find something good about your boss and your job, then you need to seriously think about going elsewhere.

Loyalty to people and mission is a character that has been lost in the workplaces of today. You should have a certain level of respect for your boss. There should be a working bond between the two of you in the workplace. You should support the mission and goals of the organization and do all you can to help see them come to pass. You should never do anything on your job to disgrace your boss or the company. I'm not suggesting that you be a doormat and ignore issues that may arise. Part of being a loyal employee is speaking up and talking to your boss when you don't agree with something. You're entitled to your opinion, but you're not entitled to always get your way. There will be times when you'll voice your concerns but nothing will change. You're still required to be loyal to your boss.

Because you committed yourself when you were hired, you're required to be faithful and defend your boss. Your boss may not have the perfection you think he or she should have, but you're still required to be faithful to your boss and to carry out your duties at work in a professional way. I'm not suggesting that you be loyal to illegal, immoral, and unethical things. You must be faithful before you can be loyal. Being offensive and non-compliant about everything your boss does is disrespectful, disloyal, and unprofessional. It's not easy being faithful when you know you're being taken advantage of. It's not easy being faithful when you know you're being used. It's not easy being faithful when you feel like quitting and walking out. But I've learned that faithfulness is something one develops, while loyalty is an act.

To be faithful is to believe in something or someone. Loyalty is something we choose to do. Faithful employees show up to work every day, while loyal employees get to work early and stay late. Just remember; you may be in a leadership position someday, and you'll depend upon the loyalty of your employees when times are hard. Most of the time, these are just tests that we are required to pass to move through the valley that we find ourselves in. Continue being faithful and loyal. There's a moral and ethical escape for every temptation.

As a school security officer, you can show professionalism by making sure you look and act the part. I don't mean looks as in appearance, such as having a clean uniform and shined shoes, even though appearance is very important; but looking as though you know what you're doing. Our body language can play a major role in how our employer and those we serve view us a being professional or not. We must show people that you can perform confidently. People will see us as someone who has the answers to safety and security issues in our school or wherever we're serving. Students in particular are watching to see how we perform on the job. Many of them may not have the first clue what professionalism looks or acts like, or what our job is, but they'll still judge us on how we handle safety and security issues related to the school.

Professionalism is demonstrated not only in how we look in action, but also in what we say and don't say. In my early days in the military, I learned quickly that most times, my opinion did not matter. Many times, I thought certain things should have been done a certain way, but I was never asked what I thought. I quickly learned the hard way that it was better not to think out loud and to keep my opinions to myself. It was better to remain silent and not take issue with every situation that I was not totally one hundred percent in agreement with. My thoughts and opinions were not important, at least not to the person or people I thought I should share them with. The important thing was that I showed professionalism as a soldier by listening, remaining silent, and doing what I was told to do. I find these principles are also true when working as a school security officer. Because I had more than one boss, I had to use discretion when speaking in certain situations. One boss may be okay and not take issue with my comments, while another one might.

At my last school, there were six principals: one head principal and five vice-principals. My job was to try to satisfy all six of them in the way I conducted myself and in carrying out my duties. If you're thinking about becoming a school security officer, one of the traits in becoming a good one is *learning to be silent and learning to speak briefly, only after you're asked to speak.* You must learn to leave school business to school principals. It's not your responsibility, duty, or business what discipline a student receives for a school violation. I've witnessed school security officers question school administrators about the type and extent of discipline issued to a student. This is bad for a school security officer, because we will not win this battle. On top of that, we would have just violated the most significant of all ethic codes—professionalism. This is not the time to show how smart you are or how much you think you know. School security officers are placed in schools to serve the administration, staff, teachers, students, and any visitors, including parents, that come on school property. I want to stress this point to all school security officers everywhere. If we ever get to the point where we start to think otherwise, we must change course and refocus. I've heard our chief of school security say to us many times as a department that we are "service support personnel." We are in the schools to support and serve. To support principals in making sure their schools are safe and secure, and serve them in the daily tasks of doing this. This principle would also apply to any security company, not just school security.

This takes me to my last area of professionalism—living up to your commitment. School security officers should have one main commitment—to serve and protect their school. Serving can cover a variety of areas, such as living up to your word, being at the place you're told to be at, being on time at completing your assigned tasks, and doing these things with a positive mental attitude. Don't be a lazy, unreliable, complaining employee.

I didn't feel completely professional in every one of these areas every single day, but I always reminded myself that I was there to serve and protect, and that I had committed myself to perform duties and responsibilities as a school security officer. I learned that if I did not commit myself to professionalism, I did not always manifest professionalism. Practicing professionalism might help keep you employed a lot longer.

Notes

Notes

CHAPTER TWELVE

A School Security Officer Must Set High Standards for Himself or Herself

It's important to have a set of standards in place for any job we undertake. Standards help provide a mental picture of what is expected in behavior and performance of any task, deed or operation. There were standards in my home when I was growing up, and there are standards in my home today. There were standards all the way through my school days and college that I was expected to live and operate by. Organizations, companies, or individuals set standards as rules and guides they hope will be followed. I got my biggest lesson in standards while I was serving in the United States Army. The military has a specific, high set of standards defining how operating procedures should be completed. In the army, these are called Standard Operating Procedures.

Chances are the organization or company where you work has a set of standards that they require you, as an employee, to operate under. Failure to meet these standards could mean missing a promotion, or worse, termination of your employment. Every school security officer should strive to meet and maintain the standards set by your employer or boss. There may be times when these standards will be revised or changed, and it's the responsibility of each individual officer to make the necessary adjustments.

Meeting or exceeding set standards is always my goal wherever

I'm employed or whatever I'm doing. Being employed as a school security officer is no different. It's important for me to set my duty and responsibility standards higher than those set by my employer. For example, my employer's standard for a normal workday shift was starting at eight and ending at four. I set a higher personal standard for myself, which required me to arrive at least fifteen to thirty minutes before the standard start of my workday, and not to depart the school building until after 4:00 p.m. It's important to mention that when I entered the school building each morning, I was ready for business. Mornings are a very busy time in schools. This is when buses and parents are dropping off children, student drivers fill the parking lot, and many children go to early classes or for tutoring. I couldn't wait until eight to arrive at work and expect to establish and maintain proper safety and security. I needed to arrive before the start of my shift to be the first one in place where a large number of students would gather.

I'll be the first to admit that I didn't always live up to some of the higher standards I set for myself, but when I didn't, I wasn't discouraged; it made me more determined to do better the next day. I never lowered the bar of standards that I had set for myself. By doing this, at a minimum, I met the set standards of my employer or supervisor. Practicing this behavior has help kept me employed at every job I've held.

When I fail to set higher standards for my own personal performance, I fail to give myself the opportunity to improve and get better at what I do on a daily basis. School security officers should always strive to make their school safer today than it was yesterday. To achieve this means not settling simply for the minimum requirements, but raising personal standards. This takes commitment, which leads into the next chapter.

The standards you set as a school security officer while on the job should be the same standards you set for yourself while off the job. The behavior you exemplify while in uniform should be the same behavior you live by while out of uniform. When people get to know you as one who has been charged with safety and security of children, they put a spotlight on you. While the spotlight is always shining, it shines brighter at some times than others. I've noticed that whenever I'm out in public and a parent recognizes me as their child's school security officer, he or she takes special interest in what I'm doing and who I'm with. I've seen some of these parents at school and they never say a word to me. But when we meet in public, they quickly identify me as the school security officer at their child's school. Many of them will go out of their way and make it a point to speak to me by addressing me as "Officer Puckett." I've run into students who will do the same. When I see this happening, I return the respect by stopping and having a brief conversation with them. I've never seen many of these parents before, but they know that I'm the school security officer at the school where their child attends.

It's important that I conduct myself professionally and show the same respect in public that I do when I'm at school. It's not the uniform or the school building that causes me to set high standards for myself, but rather the work ethic in me. If I didn't care, then it wouldn't matter where I was, what I was wearing, or what I was doing. My high standards are a part of my lifestyle. As a school security officer, it should be part of yours too. People are watching you when you think they are not.

I will tell a student a saying that when he or she gets caught doing something wrong, "Always do the right thing even when you *think* no one is watching." Someone is always watching. I'm not suggesting that you go around looking over your shoulder everywhere you go. If your standards for doing the right thing are always a high priority, then it shouldn't matter who is watching. One of my goals as a school security is to meet standards, but also to strive to exceed expectations.

Notes

CHAPTER THIRTEEN

A School Security Officer Must be Committed To High Standards

After setting those high standards, now it's time to go to work in meeting them. This requires commitment. In today's society, it's sometimes difficult to find people who will commit, and then follow through on their commitment to see it fulfilled. Commitment is a term not talked about in the workplace too often. In the minds of many people, the word "commitment" takes on the same meaning as the word "submit." Some people will not submit to anything or anyone. Likewise, some people will not commit to anything or anyone. The ones who are not committed go through their life putting out fires that could have been prevented if there had been a level of commitment at the start. When commitment is applied to our profession, standards are not only met, but are often exceeded.

School security officers must always be committed to their duties and responsibilities. Commitment is a never-ending task. Without commitment to see a task or mission to its completion, it's a failed task or mission from the start. To be committed is pledging to do whatever it takes within our scope of authority, and within the law, to get the job done. School security officers have a job to do—the safekeeping of children. Without the commitment of the school security officer to establish and maintain safety and security at our school, the school and everyone there becomes a greater target for something tragic to happen. Where there's no commitment, there's no attention to details.

At the two high schools I worked full time, I was committed to doing my best in keeping children and staff safe while they were on campus. Several times throughout the day, I would roam the school buildings and look over the parking lots, looking for any signs of unusual behavior or activity that could result in a school security breach or trouble. I committed myself to observing students' demeanors at the start of every school day and continued that watch throughout the course of the day. I particularly committed myself to keeping a watchful eye on certain students. While I wasn't following their every move, I made sure they knew I was observing them between classes. I learned that students reveal a lot about themselves through their actions and behavior.

I extended this commitment to every principal, teacher, and support staff member as well. I never put my commitment toward them down on paper, but every chance I got, I'd let them know verbally and by my actions that I was committed to their safety and security while they were at school. I hope that each and every one of them came to work each day and went about their job with peace of mind, knowing that I was committed to keeping the school safe and secure. My commitment did not stop with school personnel, but extended to parents and visitors also. If my commitment was to keep the school safe and secure, then that meant everyone who came on campus or entered the school building. Commitment has a beginning—you, the school security officer—but has no ending when it comes to the safety and security of our children.

Commitment is something that we does or doesn't do. I've heard people say, "I almost committed" or "I committed a little." We don't *almost* commit, or commit *a little*. It's all the way or nothing. We can commit in many ways, but it starts with showing up and being visible. *If you don't make yourself visible, it's just like you're not there.*

Pledge to being a person of commitment to your duties and responsibilities in keeping your school safe and secure. Commitment might mean that you have the liberty at times of delegating a portion of your duties. As the school security officer, delegation of duties doesn't free you from being responsible for them. When you're committed to a cause or a person, it brings out the loyalty in you. Without commitment, there is no loyalty. Without commitment to your service as a school security officer, there's no reliability, dependability, steadfastness, trustworthiness, allegiance, constancy, or faithfulness to your duties and responsibilities, or to those you serve.

Notes

CHAPTER FOURTEEN

A School Security Officer Must be Self-Disciplined

I intentionally saved this chapter for last because our discipline is the driving force behind the willingness to do anything. When I think about being disciplined, I'm immediately taken back to my years in the military. When I first joined the military, I had already learnt about discipline, because my parents believed in teaching and training to mold and make me into the man I am today. They believed in punishment when I did not exemplify the behavior they had taught me and expected me to live by. Their goal was to train me how to maintain self-control to do the right thing at the right time.

When I joined the United States Army in 1975, discipline took on a new meaning for me. Not long after joining, I realized that I was required to learn and maintain a level of discipline that I had never experienced in my life. Discipline in the military was somewhat easier for me than others because I had been introduced to it by my parents and other authority figures, such as teachers, grandparents, aunts, and uncles. Just as my parents taught me discipline as a child and expected me to act and live that way, likewise, after a period of time of being taught discipline by the military, I was expected to practice self-discipline throughout the rest of my military career, if I chose to have one. For example, when I arrived at basic training, I was disciplined on what to do and what not to do. I was disciplined on when to go to bed and when to get up. I was disciplined on how to manage my time and to be on time. I was disciplined in all areas in which I was expected to conduct myself on a daily basis, both while attending basic training and throughout my military journey. People made sure I experienced the maximum level of disciplinary training because their life, my life, and the lives of others depended on it.

There came a time later in my basic training when I, as an individual or as part of a group, was given the chance to prove that discipline had become the major force behind all the things I had been trained to do. We were given more freedom to do things on our own, and were expected to conduct ourselves with discipline. Our lives suddenly changed from being taught discipline to being self-disciplined. School security officers must be willing to be taught in discipline and practice self-discipline in performing their duties and responsibilities. It does little or no good for us to be taught discipline if we never advance to self-discipline.

Self-discipline is a choice. Even though our leaders and trainers in basic training were confident that they had trained us adequately in the discipline of the military ways of living, they knew it was important to give us the opportunity to practice self-discipline. From this point on in my military career, it became a matter of choice. Practicing self-discipline is always a choice, and is our own responsibility. It was my choice and responsibility to live a lifestyle that was pleasing and acceptable to the United States Army.

Every day, school security officers have the choice to do what is right and acceptable according to their employer's training, teaching, and policies. If school security officers have a problem being self-disciplined, they'll have difficulty in becoming a good school security officer. As a school security officer, I had to be self-disciplined in many areas. Examples include arriving to work on time; being where I was expected to be or needed to be; dealing with issues in a prompt, professional manner; and making sure students were aware that I was somewhere close by at all times. Showing up in the lunchroom after hundreds of students have already arrived is asking for trouble. Because many students don't always conduct themselves in a positive way, it was important that I was there at the time they were assembling for lunch. Only when my services were required in others places in the school did I not arrive at the lunch room before or at the same time they did. It was important for them to see me as they arrived. Remember: *If you don't make yourself visible, it's just like you're not there.*

Without the desire, there's no self-discipline. Without desire to arrive at school fifteen or thirty minutes before my daily shift starts, there's no self-discipline to do it. Without the desire to do my best at my duties and responsibilities, the self-discipline is not there to do my best. Displaying self-discipline always starts with a desire to do something to the best of our ability. Once the desire is there, then we must be willing to work at self-discipline. In the words of Robert Frost, the great American poet, "The world is full of willing people; some willing to work, the rest willing to let them." School security officers must be willing to do the work they were hired to do. Their work must be approached with self-discipline.

Notes

Conclusion

I've had almost as much fun writing this book as I've had working as a school security officer for the past eight years. I can say without any reservations that I've always done my best with the resources available to me. I've done my very best to promote safety and security for the students, staff members, and everyone who visited the school I was assigned to. My goal has been to create peace in and around the school so that students and staff members feel a sense of security, and I hope I've done just that. School security officers have a tremendous responsibility. They have been graced with the privilege of protecting one of God's greatest creations—children.

One final thought: I've contributed three things that made me a good school security officer (and as I write this book, I hope I'm becoming an even better one). First would be my sensitivity to all issues related to safety and security. Second is my willingness to make a conscious effort to follow through. And third, but not least, is the willingness to accept and receive the help and counsel of those I work with.

I take my job seriously. I realize that thousands of children, staff members, and parents depend on my ability to be aware of what is going on. I've made it a personal commitment to act on every tip or complaint given to me by students, teachers, principals, staff members, and parents, no matter how small or insignificant it may seem. I learned that some tips and complaints needed quick and precise attention. With the support of the administrative staff, I've done my best to make sure that every tip or complaint was dealt with or addressed. It's not my decision to make on what is legitimate or not or what is important or not; my job is to process the information and act on it the best I know how, with the appropriate help. I guess I have my parents and my military training to thank for my promptness and attention to detail at the things I'm responsible for. These are character traits of the mind. This is who I am.

Developing your work ethic may be an area that you'll have to work on diligently. A good, strong, persistent, and consistent work ethic is hard to find in most people these days. From observing people over the years, I've learned that you won't have to look for a good, strong, persistent, and consistent work ethic in people, because it will make itself visible. If your work ethic is not at the level you would like it to be, there's only one person who can change that—*you*. A work ethic is an individual responsibility and decision. You have to address tasks consciously and intentionally at the time they need to be done. You can be told and even given hands-on instructions on how something works or how it should be done, but without individual effort, your work ethic toward *that* will never materialize.

The safety and security of our schools is everyone's responsibility. Everyone, whether or not they have a child attending public schools, should be concerned about keeping our schools safe. Reporting any suspicious activities and people is imperative in helping keep schools safe. School security officers have the great responsibility of making sure their school is a safe place for children to come and learn. No person wants to have his or her name used in the same sentence with the word *bad*, in a negative way. Likewise, no school security officer wants to be known as a *bad* school security officer. They want to be known as a *good* school security officer on the way to being a *better* one. Strive to be that school security officer daily on your job. Whether it's be making sure doors are locked, maintaining crowd control, correcting students' negative behavior, making yourself visible, directing traffic, establishing and maintaining peace, or whatever the day brings, do it with pride.

School security officers are the first line of defense against any and all threats toward the school. We are the first responders to any incident that occurs at our school. If every school security officer approaches their duties and responsibilities with promptness, willingness, and readiness, people will think twice about creating trouble at their school. So, whether you're securing exterior doors, patrolling the hallways, monitoring crowd control, directing traffic, writing reports, or maintaining order, do it with promptness, willingness, and above all, readiness. Above everything a school security officer is tasked to do, our primary duty is the safety of the children at the school where we work. As long as you are a school security officer, it should be who you are, and not just what you do. Be the best that you can be.

Thank you,
James E. Puckett
United States Army, CWO4, (RET)

Notes

Contact James Puckett on the Web at:

www.jamespuckett.com

Additional copies of *A School Security Officer: What Makes A Good One* are available from your local bookstore, Amazon.com, Barnes & Noble or at www.jamespuckett.com